Reading God's Word to others

John N.M. Wijngaards
M.H.M.

MAYHEW-MCCRIMMON
Great Wakering Essex

First published in Great Britain in 1981 by
MAYHEW-MCCCRIMMON LTD
Great Wakering   Essex   England

ISBN 0 85597 315 3

Edited by Robert B Kelly
Illustrations and lithographic artwork by Graphitti
Cover design by Paul Shuttleworth
Typeset by JJ Typographics Ltd
Printed by Mayhew-McCrimmon Printers Ltd

CONTENTS

FOREWORD

This book was written to help all those
who read Sacred Scripture to others:

In order to be a good reader
we need to know certain facts.
And we need to learn some practical rules and techniques.
The suggestions contained in this book
have been tried out in practice.
They will help to make our reading effective.

However,
we would be seriously mistaken
if we believe that the practicalities
are the most important thing we need to learn.
They are not.
What we need most of all is a basic insight,
a conviction,
an attitude
that will make our reading genuine from within.

There is a difference
between a well-trained draftsman and an artist,
between a slick salesman and a witness,
between a learned theologian and a prophet.
What is the use of being an "efficient" lector
and not a witness, a mystic and prophet
at the same time?

One more remark.
Principles of theory will be illustrated
with examples taken from life.

And life is not all serious.

Only the humble man can laugh at himself.
Only faith can witness.
Only life can communicate life.

'Lord
let your word endow me with perception!'
(Psalm 119:169)

INTRODUCTION

INTRODUCTION

When you are called upon to read in Church, rejoice. Be happy. Feel proud. Just as others in your community may be ministers of the eucharist, and assist in distributing Holy Communion, so too you are entrusted with the sharing of God's Word. Through you people will have the opportunity to receive the Word that gives them light and life. God is asking that through your voice he may speak to his people.

Of course, it is not only through the liturgy of the Word that God's people share that saving Word. There are many parallel situations — in prayer groups, in teaching contexts — where God chooses to rely on you to make his message heard.

Reading God's Word to others, then presumes you are to read scripture to others, and is intended as an encouragement to you to accept that invitation to share God's Word which comes, through the Church, from God.

A not unnatural reaction to such an invitation is to hesitate, to feel wary, unsure of getting involved. By way of answer to such feelings, let me present an adaptation of a parable which Kafka tells in his book *The Process*.

Before the Bible a guard kept watch. One day an ordinary man came up to him and asked permission to read the Bible. The door leading to the Bible was open, but the guard replied he could not give permission to enter. The man hesitated, and then asked if he might be allowed to enter later. 'Perhaps,' the guard replied, 'anyway, not now.' As the guard was standing somewhat aside, the man bent over and tried to look into the interior of the door. The guard noticed this and laughed; 'If you feel tempted to go inside in spite of my prohibition, well, go ahead. However, I must warn you — you see how strong I am, and I am only the lowest guard. If you go inside, from hall to hall, you'll find other guards, the one more terrible than the other. I myself simply can't bear looking some of them in the face.'

The man had not expected such difficulties. He had always thought the Word of God should be accessible to everyone. But looking once more at the guard, his long nose and black beard, he decided it was better to wait until he got permission. The guard gave him a little stool to sit on, next to the door. There the man sat for days and weeks and years. Often he asked to be allowed in, but to no avail. He started using up everything he had taken along. He gave many presents to the guard to make him change his mind. The guard accepted these gifts 'so that you may be satisfied that you have done your best and have not omitted any chance.' But still the guard would not allow him in. For many years the man observed the guard who seemed the only obstacle in reaching God's Word. He cursed the guard, at first loudly, then bitterly . . . Slowly he became an old man. He had used up all his provisions. His clothes were worn out. His limbs bent with age. His eyesight faded and everything around him became dark. But, looking towards the doorway, he seemed to discern clearly a strong light, flooding out into the dark from the doorway.

One day the man was so exhausted he knew death was at hand. In his weary head one thought came up and took shape. It was a question he had never asked the guard before but which seemed to him all important just now. He beckoned the guard near, as he could no longer move. The guard bent over him and asked, 'You are almost dead. What more do you want to know?' The man whispered: 'Shouldn't everyone have access to God's Word? Is every person not anxious to hear God? How then is it possible that in all these years no one except myself has asked for permission to enter inside?' The guard said, 'No one else could go in by this door. This door was specially made for you. As soon as you're dead, I'm going to close it.'

God's Word is available to us all: in the words of Kafka's parable, there is a door specially made for each one of us.

You have been invited to be a reader: will you be like the man in the parable who allowed the guard to obstruct his way? Are you going to present excuses (for that is what the guard symbolises) for not committing yourself to God and his Word? Rather than getting involved do you prefer to sit outside, like the man in the parable, cursing the guard?

The whole purpose of this book is to help you make a positive response to the invitation to be a reader. I have begun by urging you to accept the invitation — what follows is dedicated to helping you fulfill the duties and responsibilities that go with the privilege of being a reader.

You will discover that this book falls into three parts:

*Part 1   The Liturgy
Since being a reader is above all else a liturgical ministry, this section establishes the context in which you will be fulfilling your responsibility.

*Part 2   The Reader
This section is concerned with the practicalities of competent and intelligent public reading.

*Part 3   The Text
The final section is dedicated to maximising your understanding of the text, helping you to extract as much meaning as possible for those who will hear you.

As little as you would want to be disrespectful to the sacramental body and blood of Christ, can you afford to be negligent regarding his Word. Make up your mind, therefore, to do all in your power to transmit God's message fully and worthily.

PART 1
THE LITURGY

THE LITURGY

Sacred scripture cannot be separated from the Church, and not as if the Church were a sort of museum in which the bible is preserved. Scripture is what gives the Church her very mission: it is the book preached by the Church, preserved by her, guaranteed by her, handed on by her, proclaimed, celebrated and made alive by her in the liturgy.

SCRIPTURE IN THE LITURGY

It is no accident that scripture reading has always had a prominent place in all of the Church's liturgy, East and West: no accident, because the liturgy of the Word is an integral part of all liturgy.

ROME, c.150AD

Here, for example, is the oldest account outside scripture itself, of the early Christians' eucharist. We are in Rome, around 150 AD:

'On the day named after the sun, all who live in the countryside or city assemble, and the memoirs of the apostles or the writings of the prophets are read for as long as time allows.

When the reading is finished, the president addresses us, admonishing us and exhorting us to imitate the splendid things we have heard. Then we all stand and pray . . .'

(First Apology of Justin, 67:3-5)

The text goes on to describe the specifically eucharistic part of the celebration.

Justin was a layman, and he wrote his *Apology* as a sort of open letter to explain to the non-Christian authorities what happened at Christian celebrations (there were rumours that Christians were cannibals because they ate 'flesh and blood' at their gatherings).

Justin, in the passage above, is quite clearly describing what we would call the liturgy of the Word:

—there are readings from *'the memoirs of the apostles'*: earlier Justin has explained that the Christians call the memoirs of the apostles 'gospels' (*Ibid 66:3*).

(This is, in fact, the first ever recorded use of the term 'gospels'.)

—there are clearly readings from the Old Testament — *'the writings of the prophets'*.

—this is followed by the homily, and notice particularly how the homily is an extension of the readings: the people are admonished and exhorted to imitate *'the splendid things* (a phrase very close to 'good news' which is what 'gospel' means literally) *we have just heard'*.

—the prayer of the faithful clearly follows.

There is a great warmth and richness in the simplicity with which Justin describes the liturgy of the Word — there is a great sense of familiarity, of closeness to the Word: the expression *'memoirs of the apostles'* makes it feel more personal; the memoirs are genuinely seen as the account of *'splendid things'*; the people seem to feel at home with scripture so that the reading goes on *'as long as time allows'*. Part of this familiarity was because of the situation of the early Church. It was a minority, very small in number, so that each community would be small, and close-knit — like an extended family. Everyone would be well known to each other. The model of the celebration, if you like, is a domestic one.

AFRICA c.400 AD

Two hundred and fifty years later we have another very vivid account of what the liturgy of the Word meant to the people in their celebration. By now, the Church has passed from being an often persecuted minority. There are now large numbers of Christians, and the model is no longer domestic, but institutional. The liturgy is now celebrated in 'basilicas' — buildings specifically designed for the liturgy (modelled on the large gatherings of the secular court).

THE BASILICA

The scene is Hippo, a town in northern Africa, around the year

400 AD. Augustine is the Bishop of Hippo, and let us imagine ourselves in his basilica.

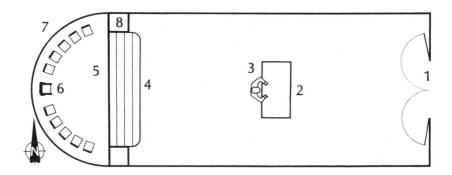

Entering the basilica by the main door (1) we find ourselves in the main body of the building, called the nave, which is about 20 yards wide and 42 yards long. In the middle of the nave is a solid stone table, the altar (2), built so that as Augustine stood there (3) presiding over the eucharist he faced east, that is, towards the door. The far end of the basilica is not a flat wall, but a semicircle: steps (4) lead up to a raised floor within this semicircle (5). On this platform or stage, Augustine has his bishop's throne, known as his *cathedra* (6) (hence the word cathedral, which means the church where the bishop has his cathedra); the platform is high enough for everyone to be able to see Augustine when he is enthroned at his cathedra. To the left and right are simpler seats for Augustine's assistant ministers i.e. his deacons and priests (7). On either side of the steps there were *'ambos')* i.e. lecterns or pulpits from which the lector and the deacon read the passages from scripture (8).

THE LITURGY

When the people gathered to celebrate mass, they congregated in the space in front of the steps (4). There, they would listen to the readings: from the Old Testament, read by a lector: from the Gospel, read by a deacon. The people stayed there to hear Augustine explain the scripture readings to them in his homily, which he gave from his cathedra (6). When the liturgy of the Word was complete, Augustine and his assistants would come down the steps; with all the people around him he would approach the altar for the celebration of the liturgy of the Eucharist.

This formal and structured arrangement contrasts with the more homely style of Justin's account, but the formality and structure have a specific purpose. No one was more aware than Augustine himself of the symbolic nature of the liturgy — he probably did more than any other theologian to help us understand the nature and meaning of the sacraments. Everything in the liturgy — words, actions, even what things are used and where — is used to make physically visible what is present as a spiritual reality. The way things are done is an expression of their meaning.

This is how Augustine himself expresses it:

'The Lord makes us holy by the power of the Holy Spirit through grace which we cannot see. But this is the result of symbols, which we can see. Without this inner sanctification through invisible grace, the visible symbols would be useless.'

(Quaestiones in Heptateuchum 3:84)

'No religion whatsoever, true or false, can be an organised, united community unless its members are bound together by common participation in visible signs (he speaks of 'sacraments'). The effect of these symbols is of unspeakable value.'

(Contra Faustum)

THE IMPORTANCE OF SCRIPTURE IN AUGUSTINE'S BASILICA

In other words, we have to see behind the arrangement of Augustine's basilica a clear statement of what is important in a liturgical celebration.

The first obvious thing is the distinct position of the table or the altar, and of the pulpit and cathedra. This helps to make very clear **the distinction between the liturgy of the Word, and the liturgy of the Eucharist.** Half way through the celebration there was the very dramatic change over, which involved everyone moving from one part of the basilica to another. Their attention was forcibly swung from one focal point (the lectern and cathedra) to another (the altar). Each focal point represented a distinct, but integral part, of the celebration: from the Word to the Eucharist.

Our present concern is with the liturgy of the Word, so let us concentrate on the appropriate areas.

The pulpit is in an elevated prominent position; the cathedra is in its own prominent position. This cannot but impress on everyone **the**

authoritative position of the scripture reading and the instruction or homily.

The importance of scripture was further underlined by a whole series of acts of reverence:

—just as the table of the eucharist was spread with a linen cloth to receive the Word made flesh, so too the lectern was draped with a linen cloth, since it supported the Word of the Lord in scripture;

—even the books of scripture themselves were held in special regard, because of their contents — they were very often highly ornamental, even with precious stones and gold fixings; there were ceremonies of incensing and greeting the book.

Because of the special place set aside for reading, with a special minister (it had to be a deacon for the gospel), and because of all the physical ceremonies that people would see and smell (incense), a real sense of the presence of God's Word was built up and was felt by the community.

We know from Augustine's own accounts that the people really did feel close to God's Word: they felt in a very real way that through his Word God was close to them, speaking to them in a way relevant to their own lives.

THE IMPORTANCE OF SCRIPTURE IN AUGUSTINE'S LITURGY

Let us picture an ordinary Sunday celebration for Augustine and his people. Augustine would begin in the sacristy, next to the basilica. He would select some readings either according to an existing tradition or according to pastoral need, and indicate these to the lector (for the non-gospel reading), to the cantor (for the singing of the psalm) and to the deacon (for the gospel reading). When everyone was vested and ready, Augustine would proceed into the basilica, greeting his people as he passed among them, ascend the steps and take his seat on his cathedra. The church would still be buzzing with the noise of the people chatting and greeting each other. The celebration began by establishing silence, which was usually a deacon's task (though at times there was so much noise that Augustine himself had to intervene to establish absolute attention and silence!). Once silence was established, Augustine would bless the lector and send him to the pulpit to begin his reading. Similarly with the cantor and deacon for their respective chant or reading.

THE EFFECT OF SCRIPTURE WITHIN THE LITURGY

From Augustine's letters and sermons we know that this reading was a real event, a genuine happening for the people. For example, in one of his homilies, Augustine is able to draw on this very real awareness of the gospel:

'When the gospel was being read, you paid great attention. As the story unfolded before you it took shape before the eyes of your heart. You saw, not with your body, but with your mind how our Lord Jesus Christ sat at table in the Pharisee's house. You saw too how a woman, renowned in the city as a sinner, gatecrashed her way in . . .'
(Sermon 49)

The people's response to the reading was vivid, because it was real for them. At times, when sin was mentioned, they would beat their breasts — a traditional sign of repentance; at other appropriate moments they would applaud and cheer their approval. They allowed themselves to be spellbound by the gospel accounts, or to be moved to prostrate themselves in prayer. These people **realised** that it was truly God who spoke to them — and they responded accordingly. In fact, those who did not participate in such responses were the exceptions, a source of scandal and indignation.

We have already noted the twofold nature of the celebration: for Augustine the sharing of the Word was of equal importance to the sharing of communion — they were both privileged moments in which God was really present and close to his people. The event was the whole liturgy of the Word — including the homily, and the whole was seen as so important by Augustine that he always gave his homily on the actual reading, even if by some misunderstanding the wrong passage of scripture was used:

'I had prepared myself for a homily on a short psalm, and had told the cantor which it was. But he seems to have got a little confused, and in fact he sang a different psalm for you. But, in this seeming mistake I see the will of God, and so I have made up my mind to follow it, rather than the one I originally had in mind.'
(Sermon 64)

THE MINISTRY OF THE WORD

Augustine considered his role in the liturgy of the Word as a 'ministry' i.e. his homily was an expanation in service of the Word that had been read. He often explicitly reminds his people that it is really God, not Augustine, that is speaking to them:

'What I say is only the means: it serves as a warning. The one who speaks to your hearts has his cathedra in heaven.'
'We are ministers of **the** Word: not our own word, but the Word of our God and Lord . . . It is the Lord our God Jesus Christ himself who says to us what we have heard just now in the gospel.'

Exactly like the liturgy of the Eucharist, Augustine sees the liturgy of the Word as an occasion of grace, a chance for a real and personal encounter with Christ. Augustine even parallels the idea of two tables: the table of the Word and the table of the Eucharist.

'In explaining the Holy Scriptures to you I am, as it were, breaking and sharing bread with you . . . What I share out with you is not my own. What you eat, I eat. What you live on, I live on. What we receive comes from the same storehouse, in heaven: that common store is the Word of God.'
(Sermon 45)

THE EFFECT OF SCRIPTURE ON LIVES

The effect the liturgy of the Word had on the hearers went beyond their response within the liturgy. The Word, properly received, had a dynamic power that literally transformed the lives of those who heard it, in a way that was visibly discernable.

In 418 AD Augustine made a pastoral visit to Caesarea of Mauritania. While there, the local bishop explained to Augustine that the city was divided into two bitterly opposed factions. On occasion this hostility erupted into physical violence where maiming and even death were not unusual. The bishop suggested Augustine might refer to this feud in his homily.

Augustine accepted, and planned the celebration accordingly. He chose texts which spoke of the need of forgiveness, and the great law of Christian love — 1 John 3:11-13, Matthew 18:23-35. For two hours Augustine then drew out the meaning and implications of God's Word as a judgement. At first the people were impressed by the beauty of the texts and thrilled by Augustine's oratory. There was long and frequent applause. Then, as understanding of what God was saying came to them, they fell silent, terrified. Finally, when they saw the promise of forgiveness, they burst into tears of repentance.

'That was the end of the feud. In the eight years since, there has been no further incidence of hostilities.'
(De Doctrina Christiana)

Augustine was aware of his responsibility as a minister of the Word: yes, the Word that was proclaimed and that he explained to his people was 'good news' for them all in a very real sense — but equally it was a Word speaking at times in judgement. It is the truth against which to measure life-style, the one true norm against which to judge actions. So, for example, when explaining Matthew 5:22 Augustine says:

'The part of the Gospel we have just heard ought to scare us stiff — if we have faith; only those who have no faith will not have been scared . . .'
(Sermon 5)
'I could say, why should I bother to be concerned about others? Why should I be telling sinners "Don't do this! Do that! Stop doing that!" What is it that makes me feel responsible for the good of others? It is because this gospel scares me . . .'
(Sermon 339:4)

There is no doubting the impact that the Word of God can have on the Christian community when it is well proclaimed and properly explained in the liturgy.

THE DARK AGES OF THE LITURGY

Sadly, the history of the liturgy shows as many examples when the Word was inadequately proclaimed, and not at all explained.

EUROPE c.800 AD

Imagine yourself at the court of Charlemagne (742-814), who had a passionate and very public Christian conviction. Having become a Christian, he set about making sure that everything, especially the liturgy, was conducted as well as possible. Here is an eye witness account of liturgical reading in the presence of Charlemagne:

'There was never anyone present in the cathedral of the most learned Charlemagne to remind each reader which passages should be recited; and when he reached the end of his own piece no one marked the place with wax or made the slightest indent with his finger-nail. They all took such care to acquaint themselves with what was to be recited that, when they were called upon to read unexpectedly, they performed so well that the Emperor never had occasion to reproach them. He indicated which of them he wished to read by pointing with his finger or his stick, or, if it was someone sitting far off, by sending a messenger from his entourage. He made it clear that he wanted the reading to stop by clearing his throat. Everyone listened very carefully for this sound. Whether it came at the end of a sentence, or in the middle of a clause, or even in a sub-clause, none of the subsequent readers dared to begin farther back or farther on, however strange the beginning or end might seem. One result of this was that *all those in the place became excellent readers, even if they did not understand what they read.*'

(From *Einhard and Notker the Stammerer. Two Lives of Charlemagne*, ed. L. Thorpe, Penguin 1969 pp. 100-101.)

The writer openly admits 'they did not understand what they read'. Yet that same document testifies to the level of technical perfection, of rubrical exactness that pervaded the liturgy of the time. The very structures which for Augustine were only the means to giving the Word due respect and honour — special ministers, the processions, use of incense, etc. — have become ends in themselves. In fact, by Charlemagne's time, there were very few people who understood the Latin of the texts; any attention they did give would be focused on the mere rubrics. Allegorical interpretation of the rubrics began to replace the explanation of the texts.

The Council of Trent did make some attempts to remove the many abuses which had crept into the way the liturgy was celebrated, and particularly in preaching However, its principal aim was to defend the doctrine on the Mass against the criticisms of the Reformers: many of the Reformer's valid proposals (for example, that the readings should be in the language of the people) were rejected because they were interpreted as part of an overall attack on the nature of the Mass and of the priesthood.

Thirty years ago or so we would have to admit that the way the liturgy was presented, and particularly the liturgy of the Word, was not immediately intelligible to the congregation present. And yet, as we have seen, for the Christians of the early centuries the liturgy, and especially the readings, were open to immediate understanding. Simply by taking part, by looking, by listening, they shared in the mysteries of God celebrated in Word and sacrament.

THE SECOND VATICAN COUNCIL

The Church was aware of this sad contrast, of how poor our liturgy seemed to be when seen alongside that of the early Church. That is why, in the person of the bishops from all over the world, the Church met in solemn Council. This we know as the Second Vatican Council — almost certainly the greatest event in the history of the Catholic Church this century.

When the bishops came together they soon discovered they shared a deep pastoral concern for the liturgy: so much so that they declared:

'the Council has special reasons for judging it a duty to
provide for the renewal and fostering of the liturgy.' *(SC 1)*

They gave this reason:

'for it is through the liturgy, especially the divine eucharistic
sacrifice that the work of our redemption is exercised.'

(SC 2)

Let us take time to think carefully about that last quotation. The Council was careful to say *'the work of our redemption* **is** *exercised'*; **not** that **we** exercise our redemption. It is God, through the Church in the liturgy, that brings redemption; salvation is his initiative; reconciliation is his free gift. It is God who calls us to himself. Therefore, the Word of God has absolute prominence in the liturgy: so the Council tells us

'The Church has always venerated the divine scriptures just
as she venerates the body of the Lord, since from the table of
both the Word of God and of the body of Christ she
unceasingly receives and offers the faithful the bread of life,
especially in the sacred liturgy.' *(DV 21)*

This understanding led the Council to make a practical demand for the renewal of the liturgy:

'Sacred scripture is of paramount importance in the
celebration of the liturgy. . . . So, if the restoration, progress
and adaptation of the sacred liturgy are to be achieved, it is
necessary to promote that warm and living love for scripture
to which the venerable tradition of both Eastern and
Western rites gives testimony'. *(SC 24)*

In other words, if we want our liturgy to have the warmth and meaning it obviously had in the time of Justin and Augustine, then we must imitate them in the way they respected and responded to the liturgical proclamation of the Word: we must imitate them first in the way we celebrate the Word that we may also imitate them in the way they responded to the Word in their everyday lives.

RESTORATION OF THE LITURGY OF THE WORD

The Council made several practical demands:
'The treasures of the Bible are to be opened up more lavishly, so that richer fare may be provided for the faithful at the table of God's Word. A more representative portion of the holy scriptures is to be read to the people over a set cycle of years'. *(SC 51)*

This was a practical demand for the restoration of the Lectionary: i.e. the official liturgical book which contains the selection of scripture texts for liturgical proclamation. The Lectionary was duly prepared to conform to the Council's wishes, and was promulgated in 1969. It is based on a three year cycle, the ordinary time of each year being dedicated to one of the synoptic evangelists. In this way Matthew, Mark and Luke in turn are our guides to the mystery of the redemption we celebrate in our liturgy.

Not only did the liturgical reform provide an improved selection of scripture extracts, but it restored the idea, so clear in Augustine's celebration, of the twofold structure of

— the liturgy of the Word
— the liturgy of the sacrament

Since Vatican II, the Mass and **all** the sacraments have been revised so that they **always** begin with a liturgy of the Word. The celebration of the Word comes first, and the rest of the celebration stands in the light of and under the instruction of the Word of God that has preceded. The Word proclaimed resounds throughout the whole celebration, and gives meaning and purpose to the rites that follow. Underlying this restoration of the liturgy of the Word is the implicit understanding that without the Word there would be no Church! It is through the Word that the incarnation became a reality; it is the word made flesh for the world of today that the Church is called to — in fact, that very call comes to the Church in the Word. This is how the Roman Missal of Paul VI expresses the role of the liturgy of the Word:

Those who gather to celebrate the liturgy are a
'. . . worshipping community, . . . the people of God, won by Christ with his blood, called together by the Lord, and nourished by his Word.' *(IGMR 5)*

That call to worship comes only through scripture — prefigured in the Old Testament and accomplished in the new; it is through the gospel that Christ's victory over sin and death is made known; it is by proclaiming the mystery of salvation revealed in scripture that the faithful are nourished by God's Word.

'. . . In the readings, explained by the homily, God speaks to his people of redemption and salvation and nourishes their spirit; Christ is present among the faithful through his Word.' *(IGMR 33)*

'. . . When the scriptures are read in Church, God himself speaks to his people, and it is Christ, present in his Word, who proclaims the Gospel.

The readings should be listened to with respect; they are a principal element of the liturgy. In the biblical readings God's Word is addressed to all men of every era and is understandable in itself, but a homily, as a living explanation of the Word, increases its effectiveness and is an integral part of the service.' *(IGMR 9)*

The purpose of the proclamation of the Word in liturgy, then, is more than providing the faithful with instruction: it is an integral part, truly the cornerstone of a full liturgical celebration.

Another consequence is that the readings have to be understood. God's Word must reach people in a way in which they can receive and assimilate it. In other words, the liturgy of the Word must be celebrated in the people's own language.

Further, the whole purpose of God's Word is to be heard, and to be understood: therefore, the reading has to be proclamation in its truest sense — it must be distinct and clear. This is no less than the right of the people of God:

'The people have the right to be nourished by the proclamation of the Word of God and by the minister's explanation of it . . .'
(Instruction on the Worship of the Eucharistic Mystery)

RESTORATION OF LITURGICAL MINISTRIES

There was one feature of Augustine's celebration that we failed to remark on, until now . . .

Notice that there was a lector; there was a cantor or psalmist; there was a deacon. Each has his own distinct liturgical role. Augustine, the bishop, does not read; does not lead the psalm: he sits and listens attentively to the readings with the rest of his people. Then he fulfils his role as the teacher of his people by his homily or instruction on the Word from his cathedra. This aspect, too, has been restored by Vatican II:

'In liturgical celebrations, whether as a minister or as one of the faithful, each person should perform his role by doing solely and totally what the nature of the liturgy demands.'
(SC 28)

This is further clarified:

'Servers, lectors, commentators, and members of the choir exercise a genuine liturgical ministry. They ought to discharge their office with the sincere piety and decorum demanded by so exalted a ministry and rightly expected of them by God's people. Consequently they must all be deeply penetrated with the spirit of this liturgy, each in his own measure, and they must be trained to perform their functions in a correct and orderly manner'. *(SC 29)*

Since Vatican II, the whole nature of liturgical ministry has been closely examined, and reformed to be truer to the genuine spirit of the liturgy. One consequence of this revision has been the abandoning of 'minor orders' as such: orders are now properly identified as only those of bishop, priest and deacon. However, as in the tradition of the early Church, Vatican II recognised that liturgical 'ministry' goes beyond the sacrament of orders: 'ministry' is an expression of our duty and privilege to take full conscious and active part in liturgical celebrations by virtue of our baptism, for by baptism we are:

'a chosen race, a holy nation, a purchased people.' *(1 Pet 2:9 quoted in SC 14)*

THE MINISTRY OF LECTOR

By virtue of our baptism we have the duty and privilege of spreading the good news of salvation: Christ's command to 'go out to the whole world: proclaim the good news' is addressed to every Christian. But among us there are some who have a special God-given talent for proclaiming his Word. The Church offers her prayer and support to such people that they may fulfill their ministry more efficiently by means of a new liturgical rite. By looking at this new rite for the installation of a lector (for such is the correct title for one who fulfils the public ministry of God's Word) we discover what the important aspects of this ministry are.

The first point to be clear about is that being a lector is a ministry on its own strength. It is **not** a stepping-stone on the road to orders. This is a specifically **lay** ministry. It is a recognition by the Church of:
1. a need for the proclamation of God's Word;
2. that this individual has a natural God-given ability to fulfil that need;
3. that the individual needs prayer and support to carry out the ministry.

A second important feature is that the rite for the installation of a lector is to be found in the *Pontifical*, i.e. the liturgical book proper to the bishop. This shows how important the ministry is in the eyes of the Church: what is happening is that the bishop is delegating the minister to assist him in his role as teacher of his people. In other words, the ministry of lector implies the reading of scripture in its fullest possible sense — which includes the task of religious instruction (e.g. of catechumens) and of preparing other temporary readers to exercise their task as effectively as possible.

This is how the rite of installation is celebrated. The bishop and his assistants enter in procession, and take their places.

After a liturgy of the Word, the rite of installation proper begins.

The candidates for the ministry are summoned by name: by responding and coming forward each candidate symbolises willingness to accept the task.

The bishop, enthroned on his cathedra, then gives a homily, which concludes with an address to the candidates in these or similar words:

'Dear sons in Christ, through his Son, who became man for us, God the Father has revealed the mystery of salvation and brought it to fulfillment. Jesus Christ made all things known to us and then entrusted his Church with the mission of preaching the Gospel to the whole world.

As readers and bearers of God's word, you will assist in this mission . . .'

Notice how the lector is seen as fulfilling his share in the preaching mission of the Church. The lector is obeying Christ's command to 'Go, teach all nations' *(Mt 28:19-20)*. So, when the lector reads, it is so that the people will hear Christ: 'Who hears you, hears me.' *(Lk 10:16)*

The bishop continues:

'. . . and so (you) take on a special office within the Christian community; you will be given a responsibility in the service of the faith, which is rooted in the word of God. You will proclaim that word in the liturgical assembly, instruct children and adults in the faith, and prepare them to receive the sacraments worthily. You will bring the message of salvation to those who have not yet received it. Thus with your help men and women will come to know God our Father and his Son Jesus Christ, whom he sent, and so be able to reach eternal life.

Here the rite is spelling out the specific task of the lector. Yes, the lector is to proclaim God's Word, but in the fullest possible sense:

—proclaiming that Word in the liturgical assembly;
—instruction on the meaning and implication of the Word especially to candidates for baptism whether adults or children;
—the ministry is to be exercised *within* the liturgy and *outside* it.

The bishop concludes his address:
'In proclaiming God's word to others, accept it yourselves in obedience to the Holy Spirit. Meditate on it constantly, so that each day you will have a deeper love of the Scriptures, and in all you say and do show forth to the world our Saviour, Jesus Christ.'

In a sense, the ministry is not given by the Church, it is merely *recognised* by the Church: the candidates are invited to accept the ministry 'in obedience to the Spirit' for this ministry is one of the gifts of the Spirit for the building up of the Church, *(cf. 1 Cor 12 & 14,* but especially *14:4 & 14:12)*

The task is not seen as a routine one, of simply being a good competent reader: the stress in the rite is not on the external performance (competence is presumed) but rather that the candidate must be personally imbued with a familiarity and love of scripture, so that the proclaiming the Word the lector can speak from the heart and communicate the inner message to others.

After the address, the bishop stands and invites all present to pray for the candidates:
'Brothers and sisters, let us ask God our Father to bless these servants who have been chosen for the ministry of reader. Let us pray that they may be faithful to the work entrusted to them, proclaim Christ to the world, and so give glory to our Father in heaven.'

After a short pause, the bishop draws the silent prayer of the people into the prayer of the Church:
Lord God,
source of all goodness and light,
you sent your only Son, the Word of life,
to reveal to mankind the mystery of your love.
Bless our brothers
who have been chosen for the ministry of reader.
Grant that as they meditate constantly on your word
they may grow in its wisdom
and faithfully proclaim it to your people.
We ask this through Christ our Lord.

Again, the prayer emphasises that the external performance is secondary, in the sense that it will flow only from the proper inner conditions.

After the prayer, the bishop sits at his cathedra, wearing his mitre: these symbolise the official nature of the act he is about to perform. Each candidate approaches the bishop, who offers him the Bible, saying:

Take this book of holy Scripture

and be faithful in handing on the word of God,

so that it may grow strong in the hearts of his people.

By his Amen and accepting the bible, the candidate symbolises his willingness to undertake the ministry.

Notice that even in these few words, as in the rest of the installation rite, the emphasis is on the spiritual dimension of the ministry.

It is not enough to proclaim the Word externally: the lector's true task is to make that Word come alive in those who listen. The lector must learn to make the scriptures meaningful and relevant. The Word proclaimed by the lector must evoke a response in its hearers: it should change them and grip them; or help them grow in faith.

The Word the lector proclaims should prove a saving Word to the hearer.

PART 2
THE READER

THE READER

In order to be a good reader of Scripture, you must first be a good reader.

READING AS COMMUNICATION

Over the past fifty years, a lot of scientific work has gone into the study of 'communication': into both its technical and its human production. Though much of the work was sponsored by governmental, military and other secular agencies, the research findings are equally applicable to communication in Church. This section attempts to summarise the key ideas that are relevant.

A. VOICE PRODUCTION

Reading is no use if the sound of the voice is not heard. Let us be very clear about this: our reading serves no purpose if the physical sound of our words does not carry to the audience. This may seem like stating the obvious, but it is a sad fact that about 45% of Scripture reading in public celebrations is lost merely on account of insufficient sound production. (This was objectively tested by experts in an experiment in a Californian diocese, cf. *Sounds Effective* by R. Clarke, Chapman, London 1969 pp. ix-x).

At the heart of insufficient sound production lies inadequate, or even wrong use of the vocal organs:
— not knowing how to 'throw' your voice properly;
— indistinct articulation;
— lack of volume.

1. KNOWING HOW TO 'THROW' OR 'DIRECT' YOUR VOICE

This is known technically as 'projecting' your voice. First of all, remember the basis of human vocal sound production:

    air comes from the lungs;

    the air is vibrated by the vocal chords in the larynx;

    the vibrating air is thrown out through the mouth.

It is the last of these three stages that has to be correct for proper voice production.

    Experience shows that three things can happen to the vibrating air:

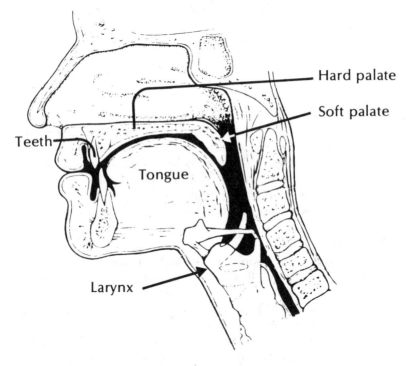

  i the sound can remain in the **larynx** (throat) with the result that it is not thrown out at all, or not sufficiently. For example, try and say 'Aaah' as deeply as you can: you will find that in being deep it automatically becomes quieter.

  ii. the sound can be thrown against the **soft palate** (the fleshy part right at the back of the roof of your mouth). For example, try making an 'Oooh' sound: you will find it difficult to make this sound strong — it tends automatically to be high and thin.

iii. the sound can be projected onto the **hard palate** (the hard part at the front of the roof of your mouth). Precisely because it strikes the hard palate, sound produced in this way is itself hard, penetrating and resonant.

In ordinary conversation, we instinctively make use of all three ways of 'sounding' — and the way we place or project the sound is relatively unimportant because the listener is near enough to catch even the larynx (throat) sounds. But when speaking to and reading for a large audience, good sound production is essential. You should try and project the sound onto the hard palate.

Speaking this way has several advantages:

a. because it is reflected off the hard palate, very little of the sound is lost, it remains strong and hard.

b. because of its position, your lips, your teeth, your head, and even to some extent your chest, act as resonators. They vibrate along with the sound and so amplify it.

c. because it is less tiring. The traditional hoarseness from loud speaking is a sure sign that the voice is not being produced far enough forward.

2. ARTICULATING PROPERLY

Vowels and consonants are the building blocks of speech, but they need to be strung together (articulated) in the right way. Bad articulation is the result of indistinct pronunciation of vowels and consonants. The commonest causes are:

— not opening your mouth widely enough;

— inadequate freedom in the movement of your lips, especially the upper lip;

— lack of proper control of your tongue muscles;

— speaking too quickly (in some people this is so habitual as to become almost a nervous habit).

3. VOLUME

'Volume' is the technical way of describing the degree of loudness in speaking.

The final volume of your speaking depends directly on the quantity of air and the force with which you emit it as you speak. The key to volume control is breathing and breath control.

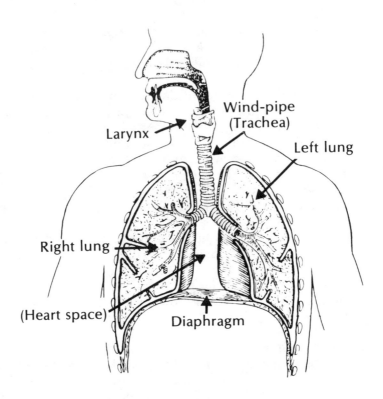

There are three ways of *breathing:*
— **collarbone breathing** where you use the contraction of your upper
  shoulders to regulate your breathing. Your lungs are pearshaped
  — narrower at the top than at the bottom, and shoulder breathing
  means you are using only the narrower upper sections. This way
  of breathing is entirely wrong since it actually prevents good and
  loud speaking — quite simply, you won't have enough breath!
— **diaphragmatic or rib breathing** where you use the contraction of
  your ribs and diaphragm to control your breathing. Your ribs
  encase your lungs, and the diaphragm is a dome-shaped muscle
  which effectively acts as the floor of your lungs. When you
  breathe in, your shoulders should not move, but you allow your
  lungs to expand outwards to fill your chest and downwards. Since
  this allows far more air into your lungs, it will greatly improve
  the amount of air you can release, and so improve your volume.
  However, by itself this form of breathing is not enough to give you
  real control of your voice.

— **abdominal breathing** is where your abdominal muscles pull down and outwards, allowing the diaphragm more room to expand your lungs to their very base. Your lungs are at their very broadest there, and yet rarely exercised. There is an easy way to test how 'deeply' (in its most literal meaning) you are breathing: press your hands into your sides at waist-level, and then breathe in deeply aiming at filling up the bottom of your lungs. If you are doing it properly, as your lungs fill downwards and sideways, your hands will be pushed out.

LUNGS AND BREATHING

These pairs of diagrams illustrate the difference that proper breathing makes to the size and shape of the lungs.

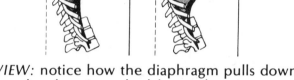

SIDE VIEW: notice how the diaphragm pulls down and how the chest is pushed forward.

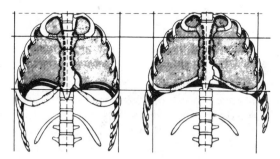

FRONT VIEW: notice how the diaphragm pulls down and how the rib cage is pushed out.

For public speaking and reading you should learn to develop abdominal breathing — and incidentally, when breathing in, breathe only through your nose. It is designed by nature not only to filter the air, but to warm it, so that it is gentler on your throat on its way back out.

It is not enough to be breathing properly, you must learn *breath control*. Your full lungs are exactly like a balloon — the compressed air will escape as fast as possible at the first opportunity. It is not easy to keep your ribs and diaphragm expanded, and as they return to their natural relaxed position, they squeeze the air out. You have to learn to control the rate at which you allow the breath to escape.

Ideally, you want to start emptying your lungs from the bottom: pulling in your abdomen, then pushing upwards with your diaphragm. Only when that is complete should you allow your ribs to contract and push the rest of the air out. (In fact, you will not be able to keep your rib cage absolutely rigid, but do not allow it to collapse!)

Good breathing, then, consists in:
— *good intake*
   the ability to inhale a good quantity of air quite rapidly and noiselessly;
   the ability to retain that air for a good period of time;
— *good outlet*
   the ability to release that air in a gradual and controlled way.
Footnote: Do not be misled into thinking that a microphone means you do not have to read loudly. Quite apart from the not remote possibility that it may not be working, the ability to speak loudly is essential for proper expression cf. p. 39.

B. VOICE REGULATION

You can regulate your voice in three basic ways:
1. **by changing the speed of speaking**, the pace, the rapidity of utterance. The fundamental speed of speaking is determined by the circumstances: how many listeners there are, how near, etc. In public speaking, it is absolutely essential to speak slowly — otherwise your voice will not carry. But within that overall minimum slowness, you can modulate your reading by varying the pace:
   —reading faster to indicate excitement;
   —reading phrases or sections more slowly to indicate their importance.
2. **by changing the pitch of your voice**, that is, by speaking higher or lower. The sound will carry better, and be easier on the ear of the

listener when it is lowish to middle. But make careful use of differentiation of pitch:

—raising the pitch normally indicates a climax;

—reading in a lower pitch suggests solemnity and seriousness.

3. **by changing the volume** at which you speak or read. Obviously, there is a basic mean volume so that all of the reading is clearly audible, but within that:

— reading more softly attracts attention;

— reading more loudly expresses conviction.

Although for convenience we have considered these ways of regulating your voice independently, they are in practice mutually related and interdependent. Most often, in natural speaking we increase speed, pitch and intensity all at the same time — so much so that if you increase one e.g. speak louder, people have the impression that you are also speaking faster.

This is known technically as the *association scale of voice modulation:*

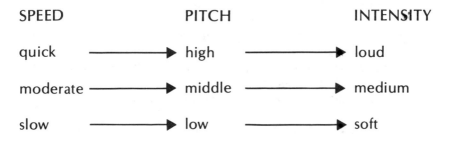

SPEED	PITCH	INTENSITY
quick ⟶	high ⟶	loud
moderate ⟶	middle ⟶	medium
slow ⟶	low ⟶	soft

People instinctively associate these three elements. But you can consciously distinguish them, with important benefits:

— when the audience is so large that you cannot speed up in your delivery, you could suggest rapidity by using a higher pitch and greater intensity;

— if you happen to have a naturally high pitched voice, you can compensate to a great degree by speaking more slowly and deliberately.

In the main, you will be regulating your voice in accordance with the meaning of the text you have to read. When you are preparing for the reading, you should prepare it as it will be i.e. aloud. Plan out the appropriate modulations of your voice, and mark the text to remind you. The following accepted symbols ought to help you:

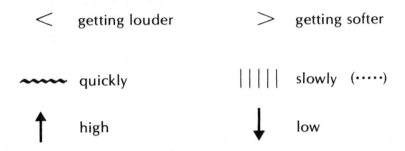

$<$ getting louder $>$ getting softer

〜〜 quickly | | | | | slowly (·····)

↑ high   ↓ low

Always remember that the hearers will not receive the message except through the sound that reaches their ears. The success of your reading depends absolutely on the quality of sound you produce. There is no point whatsoever in having a reader who cannot be heard, regardless of other good qualities that person may have.

So, for example, it is wrong to invite a prominent person to read for a liturgical celebration out of some sense of duty or etiquette if we are at the same time aware that his voice will not carry enough to be heard by everyone. Similarly, just because a particular celebration is more specifically designed for children does not necessarily mean a child should read. Audibility must take preference over sentiment.

Treat the sound which is to become the Word of God with as much respect as you do the bread and wine that is to become the body and blood of the Lord: they should be as humanly perfect as possible.

Sometimes readers feel shy about raising their voices and speaking with sufficient volume — lady teachers and sisters especially seem to have a misplaced respect which makes them read in reverential whispers. True reverence is shown by acting on God's Word, but how are people to act on it if they have not even been able to hear it? There is no need for this false timidity. Remember the importance of the task you are fulfilling: **proclaiming God's Word.**

C. PAUSES

Until now we have concentrated on the quality of the sound. In the correct transmission of sound pauses play a major role. A pause is quite simply a deliberate absence of sound. An uninterrupted flow of sound soon tires the ear of the listener. Proper placing of pause will make what you have to read easier to, and gives the sound greater relevance, i.e. makes what you say easier to understand.

There are three particularly useful ways to employ pauses:

Initial pause. It is absolutely essential to begin with a pause. Do not begin until you have captured the attention of the audience. Inexperienced readers launch into their reading immediately, with the inevitable result that the first two or three lines are lost. Wait until people are settled, and you will find them looking up expectantly: then begin.

Dividing pauses. In the written word there are any number of ways that the author can indicate divisions of thought within his material e.g. separate chapters, separate paragraphs, separate subsections, perhaps even numbered. You have to try and express the divisions of thought in the reading verbally — and your principle tool in this will be a dividing pause. It is not just a case of a uniform pause throughout wherever you note a change of thought. The length of pause should vary to express the degree of division of thought:

—the pause that divides paragraphs should be longer;

—the pause that divides sentences or thought units should be shorter;

—the pause that divides phrases (groups of words that belong together) should be only a slight retention of breath.

The punctuation marks (full stops, commas, colons, etc.) in the printed reading are a good guide, but do not follow them blindly. You should link together those parts that go together to make a unity of thought: a pause, of whatever length is suitable, marks that section off from the next section which makes up another unity of a different thought.

Stress pauses. A pause can serve to highlight the item of speech either immediately preceding or that which follows. Try these phrases and see the added impact the pause can give:

—*before a word*

'Woe to you, scribes and pharisees,
PAUSE hypocrites.'

'Do not call any man on earth
PAUSE "Father", for you have only one
Father and he is in heaven.'

—*after a word*, together with the right voice inflection (i.e. higher pitch, greater intensity, etc.)

'Two robbers **PAUSE** were crucified with him.'

'Look, I **PAUSE** am going to send my messenger before you.'

—*before and after* a word or short phrase

' "I who am speaking to you," said Jesus
PAUSE "I **PAUSE** am he." '

Just as there are symbols to stand for variation in speed, pitch and volume (cf. p. 40) so too there are shorthand ways of referring to these different sorts of pause:

> **IP** stands for initial pause;
>
> **DP** for dividing pause;
>
> **SP** for stress pause.

D. BODY LANGUAGE

So far we have treated public reading as a one-way process — we have looked at how to ensure that the sound produced by the reader is adequate in quantity and quality to reach the 'audience'. This could be symbolised by this model.

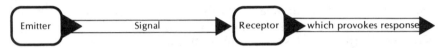

But we cannot treat public reading as a one-way transmission of sound. Yes, we have tried to ensure that the sound is loud enough and clear enough to be heard: but that, in turn, is only so that it may have a chance of being understood. In other words, we are concerned not with a one-way process, but with **communication** i.e. an interchange, which is as much between receptor and emitter as it is between emitter and receptor.

In other words, we have to amend our model to take account of the fact that part of the 'response' that the 'signal' provokes in the receptor is to send a signal back to the emitter: this second signal is known technically as 'feedback'.

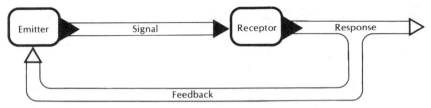

This 'feedback' can take many forms. If the model referred to a conversation or a debate, then the feedback, like the original signal, might be speech. In public reading the audience do not signal the feedback by speaking (at least not usually!). But they do react and communicate their reaction through what is called **body-language**.

Body-language is an extremely subtle way that all of us have of communicating — it is something we share with the animal kingdom, and as such much of it operates by instinct. We both give and receive messages through body-language naturally and subconsciously. Body-language is very subtle, and of its nature vague: it operates more by creating impressions. As such it would be wrong here to try to codify body-language, to try and pinpoint exact meanings to specific gestures. In fact, because it is instinctive, or imprinted on us by our particular culture, the best advice is to say simply **act naturally; be yourself**.

However, an awareness of some of the more obvious implications of how body-language operates can help in getting a reading across.

1. SPATIAL POSITION

Where you are in relation to the audience expresses your relationship with them:

—too far away suggests remoteness, aloofness, the hearers do not feel the reader forms a unity with them.

—the hearers must be able to see the reader — a seemingly disembodied voice robs the reading of its persuasive power. This rules out, for example, reading from the back of the church or chapel. It also rules out trying to hide yourself behind the lectern. In body-language this conveys an impression of shame or uncertainty.

2. STANCE

—The reader and hearers should be face-to-face, since this implies direct communication.

—our posture, in body-language serves to express the degree to which we accept each other (turning your back symbolises rejection).

—by standing erect and by not moving you indicate:
  —an impression of confidence in your ability to tell them something important;
  —that you do not expect to be interrupted.

—conversely, in sitting the hearers express receptivity and readiness to listen. If a listener turns away, it indicates he does not agree, or at least has reservations about what is being read. Restlessness indicates the message is failing to hold the hearers' attention. The highest expression of disagreement is to walk out.

3. SOUND CONTROL

One reason why we have taken so much trouble to establish good

sound control is that it, too, has a body-language function. The way you control sound, that is, the way you manipulate pauses, the pace, intensity and volume, creates certain impressions. Good sound control can express your position as a leader. Shy readers usually read fast, as if to apologise for reading at all:
—the initial pause and the stress pause punctuate the importance of the message in the body-language of the reader.
Remember, again, that communication is an interchange, and we need to look for sound control in the hearers:
—perfect silence indicates that the message has struck home;
—coughing, shuffling of feet and other such noises, however small, indicate indifference, and failure to make contact.
A good reader will be sensitive to the feedback this body-language provides, and will know to try to re-establish contact, for example, by reading more slowly, articulating more carefully, speaking more deliberately.

4. MOUTH SIGNALS

In the animal kingdom, baring teeth is a sign of hostility, it is a threatening challenge. We humans also have a whole range of signals that can be read from each other's mouths. The way the mouth is held can convey anger, fear, tension, happiness and joy. As a reader you can help to set the atmosphere the reading may require by the right mouth signal. A little smile (**not** a grin or a laugh) can often help to relax the atmosphere. It is surprising how many readers can read about God's love with a grim and deadly serious expression, jaw set hard . . .

5. EYE CONTACT

There are a whole range of 'looks' distinguished by experimental psychology, but the most significant for our purpose are:
—**the stare**: staring is normally reserved for things, inanimate objects. Staring at someone, then, implies they are less than human. Obviously, this is totally inappropriate for reader and hearers.
—**the 'lock glance'**: closely related to staring, this means you look at someone, see them looking at you, but do not avert your eyes as you might normally. Such a glance conveys hostility and usually implies a challenge. In Mexico people are shot for looking this way: to be avoided!
—**the 'sideways glance'**: implies furtiveness, wanting to see without being seen. This can be a symptom of nervousness, but either way it will make hearers feel uncomfortable.
—**the 'politely vague look'**: this is the normal form of eye contact for

conversation. It avoids prolonged direct eye contact, but maintains enough contact now and then to create the impression of being interested in what the other has to say. In public speaking this establishes general contact: you allow yourself to gaze over the audience without looking at anyone in particular.

—the **'direct look'**: this is deliberate and sustained eye to eye contact — though it differs between listener/s and reader:

listeners normally maintain direct contact longer than the reader can — though should the reader look at them the listeners avert their gaze to indicate they are not 'staring';

readers maintain only occasional direct looks and do so either to establish direct contact at the beginning of a reading reasserting their presence or to give special emphasis to what is being read, since it implies 'I am saying something important' or 'I know what I am saying'.

—the **'looking away look'**: this has many functions. It can be used as a signal for a shift in the communication. Used by a listener it would convey anything from reservations about what is being said to boredom. When used by the reader it implies uncertainty.

Eye contact is not just useful, but a necessary and unavoidable part of communication. A good reader will be aware of the implications of how and when to look at the listeners; you need to be sure that you make eye contact in the way most conducive to the message you have to read.

6. GESTURES

Very few people make gestures while they read — but if you could see yourself when you speak (rather than read) you would probably be surprised by the extent and range of your gestures. It would be a pity, then, to exclude all notion of gesture in reading. Admittedly, there are physical restrictions: the constraint of being at a lectern; of having to hold the lectionary. Reading, though, can be enlivened by gestures. Again, rather than practising some kind of theatrical gesture, it is more a case of being aware of how you would use your body naturally and spontaneously to express the message if you were speaking it, as distinct from reading it.

One valuable overall principle is not to use gestures to underline individual words, or else the reading becomes jerky and spasmodic. Rather, gestures should underline whole sentences, or sections. So, for example, it does not take much imagination to see how this paragraph could be enlivened by a good reader:
'No one can be the slave of two masters:

he will either hate the first and love the second,
or treat the first with respect and the second with scorn.
You cannot be the slave both of God and of money.'
One final word of warning: the easiest gesture of all is the 'raised finger'. But by itself it would become limp and empty. If we use gestures at all, we should learn to use a variety of them.
We can sum up and symbolise all we have discovered in this section in a model.

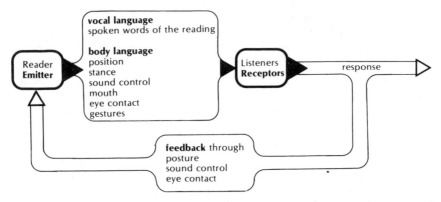

Here is an extract from a critique of a theatre production: what it says about the effective use of gesture is made doubly relevant since the production is Alex McCowen's 'St Mark's Gospel'. It is a one-man-show in which Alex McCowen presents the whole of the Gospel of St Mark (in the Authorised Version).

Mr McCowen comes before us as a man eager to tell us a thundering good story by all the means in his power. His eloquent hands describe the roof through which one sick of the palsy is lowered. His voice perceptibly thickens when a boozy Herod guiltily recalls the story of John the Baptist. As James and John ask if they may sit on the right and left hand of Jesus, they glance nervously over their shoulders in case the other disciples hear. Everything is characterised so that no shred of meaning shall escape us . . .

Through language, timing and gesture, he recaptures the first-time amazement of the living witness. In the parable of the sower he searches quizzically in the ground for the mustard-seed and then gazes skywards with rapture as it grows up. He can also instantly alter the narrative focus. When Jesus cures Jairus's daughter, Mr McCowen first of all becomes the protagonist taking the girl's hand in his and then immediately gives us the thunderstruck reaction of the lookers-on . . .

the story is creatively interpreted rather than simply rendered . . .

one feels in the presence of a chain of urgent communicators: from Jesus through St Mark to the translator of the King James version and finally to Mr McCowen himself, who comes on like a man who has just heard a fantastic story and must tell it at all costs.

(Critique by Michael Billington, *The Guardian* 12 July 1981)

PART 3
THE TEXT

THE TEXT

CHRISTIAN UNDERSTANDING OF SCRIPTURE

Sacred scripture contains the message of life: in it God speaks to man. This is and always has been a central and essential belief for the Church. That belief has been re-affirmed and restated by the Church in her official documents many times in the course of her history, most recently at the Second Vatican Council:

'Holy Mother Church, relying on the beliefs of the apostles, holds that the books of both the Old and New Testament . . . having been written under the inspiration of the Holy Spirit, have God as their author . . .

. . . it follows that the books of scripture must be acknowledged as teaching firmly, faithfully and without error that truth which God wanted put into the sacred writings for the sake of our salvation. *(DV 11)*

The key to the importance of scripture is given by that last phrase: what is important is the truth that scripture carries. Therefore, our concern must be not so much for the external word, but rather for what God has to say to us by means of that external word. For orthodox Hindus, the Vedas are inspired only in their Sanskrit form; for Muslims, the Qur'an was composed in Arabic by God himself, and so the recitation of the text must be in Arabic. Our Christian understanding of scripture is different:

'Since God speaks in sacred scripture through men in human fashion, the interpreter of sacred scripture, in order to see clearly what God wanted to communicate to us, should carefully investigate what meaning the sacred writers really intended, and what God wanted to convey by means of their words.' *(DV 12)*

The original language, the external way of saying, the form of words —
these are all ultimately immaterial: the meaning of God's Word and
the purpose of his message are what count.

THE NEED OF TRANSLATION

This very basic principle that it is the meaning behind the words
we must reach has a very important consequence. No matter what else
we may do, if we do not succeed in getting across the message, then we
have failed. To be sure that we are getting across the meaning in
scripture, we need to become expert at **translating the scripture
message.**

This process of 'translation' has many stages, which are perhaps
best illustrated by a particular example. We begin with a phrase from
the original scriptures: here is Luke 9:25 in the original inspired Greek.

Τι γαρ ωφελειται ανθρωπος κερδησας τον κοσμον ολον
εαυτον δε απολεσας η ζημιωθεις;

There is nothing sacred about the Greek itself, even though we
describe this as 'the inspired text'. In fact, since this sentence is
reported by Luke to be from the lips of Jesus, we are already one stage
removed from the spoken original: Christ would have spoken these
words in Aramaic. But because Luke is writing for a community who
speak Greek, that is obviously the language he uses. For him, quite
clearly it is the meaning that counts. Luke has quite naturally adopted
the first stage in the process of 'translation' which is **translating to one's
own language.**

Our own language is English. Here are some well-known English
versions of that same text, Luke 9:25:

Douai: 'For what is a man advantaged if he gain the whole
world and lose himself and cast himself away?'

Knox: 'How is a man the better for gaining the whole world, if
he loses himself, if he pays the forfeit of himself?'

Jerusalem: 'What gain, then, is it for a man to have won the
whole world and to have lost or ruined his very self?'

NEB: 'What will a man gain by winning the whole world, at
the cost of his true self?'

All four versions are in English, but they are not all equally
understandable. By using an expression like 'forfeit', for example, the
Knox edition seems appropriate only for a well-educated, adult

52

audience. This is precisely the second stage of 'translation': **translating for a specific audience.**

Translating for a specific audience falls into one of two major categories.

i. people who have to make a scientific, and technical study of biblical passages need to work as closely as possible to the original text in its original language. If they have to use a translation it must then be as close to the original language in style and construction as possible. We call this a **'source-oriented'** translation.

SOURCE-ORIENTED TRANSLATIONS
Douai
Revised Standard Version
Knox

ii. for most people the unusual vocabulary, the strange constructions, and the unfamiliar style become an obstacle, rather than an aid, to understanding. It is far preferable that they have a translation which uses the words, idioms, expressions and style to which they are accustomed in everyday life. We call this a **'receptor-oriented'** translation.

RECEPTOR-ORIENTED TRANSLATIONS
New English Bible
Jerusalem Bible
Today's English Version

Here is a simple example to illustrate the difference. Let us take the parable of the unforgiving servant in Matthew 18:23-35. A **source-oriented** translation reads:

'One was brought to him who owed him 10,000 talents' *(RSV).*

A **receptor-oriented** translation reads:

'One of them was brought in who owed him millions of pounds' *(TEV).*

Since the task of a reader is to make God's Word as accessible as possible to all those who will hear you, as a general rule your interest will be in receptor-oriented translation. For your own personal study you might find recourse to source-oriented translation necessary from time to time, but for pastoral use the translation ought to be receptor-oriented.

Nor should this surprise us: it follows from the very nature of scripture itself. From the very beginning the sacred authors have tried to communicate God's message in the way they thought best suited to their contemporary audience.

In an enquiry on vocations a religious sister wrote: 'I got the idea of becoming a religious from those words of our Lord, "What do you gain by winning the whole world if you suffer damage to your own soul?" What she wrote is immediately identifiable as the words of Christ from Luke 9:25 — but they are expressed in a very personal way. Personal, not just because she has put it into her own words, but that she was able to put it into her own words because it meant something for her life. She had actually decided to become a nun on account of it: for her it had become an invitation from Christ to her personally to dedicate herself to the religious life. This is an example of the third stage in the process of 'translation': **translating to the reality of life** — which often expresses itself in being able to 'say it in your own words'.

The need of translation has a second and very important consequence: in this process we must never forget that we are merely translators. We are not preaching our own philosophy. It is not we who endow the text with meaning, our task is rather to work at discovering the message that the text somehow carries. In other words, we have to be faithful to what God is saying:

'. . . holy scripture must be read and interpreted according to
the same Spirit by whom it was written . . . *(DV12)*

Yes, we have to translate scripture passages as fully as possible: but we must never lose sight of the original, for that is the key to the meaning of the passage,

QUEST FOR MEANING

In order to be faithful to the inspired message when seeking out its meaning it is essential that we have a clear idea of how meaning is conveyed by writing, and by the use of language. Modern studies can help us a lot in understanding how it is that texts carry meaning. There are three main sources of such insight:
1. linguistic studies
2. literary analysis
3. theology of revelation

1. LINGUISTIC STUDIES

Quite obviously, when we communicate through language, whether spoken or written, we do so not by manipulating the objects or actions themselves directly; somehow we do it indirectly through the medium of language. It remains to clarify what that 'somehow' is.

a. the 'notional' theory of meaning

One way of trying to understand how meaning operates is to think of it in a sort of mechanical way: in language we do not manipulate objects themselves directly, but we do so by means of mental notions or concepts: each concept has a corresponding word in language which enables us to talk meaningfully.

This is an eminently simple model of meaning, and with varying degrees of sophistication was the theory held by the early Greek philosophers, and later the scholastics. They believed that the mind somehow grasped objects and actions by the means of concepts which were contained in particular words. The mechanical way in which much foreign language teaching, now more common than ever before, is conducted may lead many people to unconsciously adopt such a literalist understanding of meaning. A preference for word-for-word translation, for example, is a symptom of such an understanding (that there is only one concept, therefore all you have to do is find the right word to contain it in whatever language).

Such an understanding of how meaning operates is at best inadequate, and at worst is liable to hinder clear and effective communication.

b. the 'referential' theory of meaning

The notional theory falls down in taking words themselves as the basic unit of meaningful communication. Meaning does not reside in individual words; nor is it contained in complete phrases or sentences. Meaning can only result from a total unit of communication, from everything that was said by a person in a particular context. Once we accept that the basic unit is the total experience we can begin to see more clearly the role that words themselves play.

Words do **not** contain concepts; they refer to them. Words are like handles by which we get a hold of a certain experience.

Here is a simple example which illustrates this, by showing how different languages may use different handles to refer to the same experience :

the diagram depicts an object which
in English is called *umbrella*,
    derived from the Latin *umbra*, which means *shade;*
in French is called *parapluie*,
    literally *against rain;*
in German is called *Schirm*,
    which stands for *protective cover;*
in Telegu is called *godugu*,
    a term related to the word for *gift*, because of popular belief that it
    was presented by the gods to give relief to mankind;
in Malay is called *pajong*,
    which seems to be a reference to its shape.
These terms are obviously related and may at times refer to the same
experience — in which case we could substitute one term for another in
translation. However, it should be equally obvious that these terms are
not truly synonymous, not strictly identical in their meaning. So:
in English we may say that some congress was organised *under the
umbrella* of this or that institution;
in German, *Schirm* may also be used to refer to a parachute;
the Malay *pajong* may be used by the Balinese to refer to a ceremonial
    'umbrella' which has no European equivalent.

Here is another example. Let us imagine ourselves in an
equatorial country at the height of summer. We are sweating profusely
and in consequence our skin is itchy and irritated. In English I might
describe this as *prickly heat;*
a Dutchman would call it *rode hont* — literally *red dog;*
in Telegu it would be called *chemata kaya* — literally *the fruit of sweat.*
These three expressions are synonymous to the extent that they mean
the same thing. But notice what is happening in each language:
in English the experience is characterised by the sensation;
the Dutch expression refers to the appearance of the red inflamed skin;
the Telegu expression indicates it by its cause, excessive sweating.
It would be incorrect to say that any one of these expressions by itself
contains the totality of what we experience. In each case, whatever

language is used, by referring to a prominent part of the experience, the total experience is recalled in our mind.

Words, then, are merely instruments, the means by which we refer to experiences. The connection between words and the objects and experiences they help us to identify is purely arbitrary — as a glance at the history of any language will show.

That words are merely instruments is seen most clearly in our ability to speak metaphorically. If I use the noun 'fox' in certain contexts, you will conjure up a mental picture of the reddish-brown dog-like animal ... and yet exactly the same word in a different context will refer not to an animal but to a person, because I am alluding or referring to certain qualities that traditionally we observe in the animal. Or I might say: 'He foxed me at every occasion'. 'Fox' has now become a verb, used to refer to a style of action. By using the word I am conveying the stealthiness, and usually the trickery that we associate with the animal in the first instance. Those connotations or overtones are being used to refer to an experience of an individual's behaviour.

We must conclude, therefore, that words do not have 'notional' meaning (they do not contain meaning), but have 'referential' meaning (They refer to an experience which is thereby recalled in our minds).

This has very important consequences for the whole process that we have described as translation. It means that translation is not concerned with a word-for-word replacement by equivalents in other languages. Once you recognise that words are only the instruments by which we refer to experiences, the question for the translator becomes, 'what instruments can I use to be true to that same experience?'.

Let us take a small biblical example. In Mark 7:6 we find:
'This people honours me with their lips,
but their heart is far from me.'
What we find in the original Greek text is an exact literal translation of the Hebrew — for Mark here is quoting Isaiah 29:13. In this short sentence there are two words in particular that we might give thought to if we are to verify whether we are grasping the experience the author intended to convey, that is, to be sure we are taking the correct meaning:

'lips': the original Hebrew uses the concrete noun 'lips' to convey the abstract notion empty external words which carry no real inner conviction. It so happens that in English we have the same idea — we speak of 'lip-service'. In Assamese, however, these overtones are connected not with the lips, but with the tongue.

'heart': in a similarly concrete way, Hebrew uses the word for the physical organ to refer to our abstract emotional nature. It is used to

cover the whole range of what we might call sensitivities. Again, the English idiom has a similar usage, where the heart is interpreted as the seat of feelings and emotions, and so comes to stand for those feelings. In Assamese however, the experience of love is referred to as being sited in the liver.

Consequently, the same meaning of the original Gospel passage is conveyed by totally different words, precisely because these words point to the same experience:
in English:
'This people honours me with their *lips,*
but their *heart* is far from me.'
in Assamese:
'This people praises me with their *tongue,*
but their *liver* is really far from me.'

When reflecting on the meaning of a biblical passage, then, we should not lose ourselves in terms or in words. Rather, we should think of the passage itself, or the expressions in it, as referring to an original experience. We have to try and recreate this same experience through our use of our own language — then we are truly bringing out the meaning of the passage. It is not the actual words that count, but the underlying experience that is pointed at through the words.

2. LITERARY ANALYSIS

There was a time when literary analysis was reduced almost exclusively to grammatical sentence construction. We were taught how to construct a sentence so that it had meaning. Again, underlying this there was a sort of mechanical understanding of meaning: words were the building blocks of meaning, which had to be arranged, or constructed according to set grammatical rules. As long as you adhered to the rules, you would have a meaningful sentence.

Modern analysis has shown such an approach to be fallacious. Philosophically, its principal fault is that it confuses 'sense' and 'meaning'. The rules of sentence construction can do no more than produce sentences which seem to make sense; thereafter whether or not they have meaning and what that meaning may be is another question. Bertrand Russell demonstrated this with his 'trick' sentence 'The present King of France is bald'. Because this is a properly constructed sentence from a grammatical point of view, it may at first seem to have meaning. In fact, you cannot even begin to ask whether it is meaningful because it purports to refer to someone who cannot be referred to!

Even without the subtleties of philosophical analysis, the ever-improving study of literature has shown how inadequate and misleading it is to treat sentences as if they contain meaning. Let us take a simple biblical example: if you were to take the sentence as the basic unit of meaning, then you will find that scripture says 'There is no God'. What matters is not the sentence by itself, of course, but the context, or the literary form, in which the sentence occurs. In other words, we should have read:

'The fool says in his heart,
"There is no God!" *(Psalm 14:1 & Psalm 53:1 JB)*

The context now makes it clear that rather than making a definite statement that there is no God, scripture is asserting exactly the opposite. Without the context, or literary form in which the sentence occurs we can say nothing certain about its meaning.

The literary form of that simple example was a small compact unit — but the context or literary form may operate on a larger scale. Take *Luke 16:19ff.,* for example. Jesus says:

'There was a rich man who used to dress in purple and fine
linen and feast magnificently every day. And at his gate
there lay a poor man called Lazarus, covered with sores . . .'
(JB)

Jesus' words are reported in a very matter of fact way, all the way through to verse 31: he seems to be talking about two historical characters, the luxurious life of the rich man, the misery of Lazarus, and so on. In fact, Jesus is not talking about two historical characters, nor a real historical event. All of these seemingly exact references go together to make up a total unit which has a literary form known as *a parable.* A parable is a narrative intended to illustrate one truth. In this important sense parables differ from allegories, because parables should be interpreted as one single unit: the various elements are not meant to convey separate meanings. The individual sentences, statements and descriptions, then, are merely elements. They cannot be understood except in terms of the parable as a whole. These additional details merely add colour, make the parable more lively, more interesting. Parables only have one central meaning.

When looking for meaning in a scripture text, then, we must first ensure that we respect the literary form in which it is presented to us by the author. We have to look for meaning in the literary units as a whole, and not through individual words or even isolated sentences. We should be asking, what is it that the literary unit as a whole is trying to convey to me?

This meaning of the literary unit as a whole is what we call the

fundamental assertion. For example, the fundamental assertion of the parable in *Luke 16:19-31* is 'Share your riches with the poor'. This basic central truth is expanded through the imagery of the two characters and their interplay — but these are all secondary elements adduced in support of the central and fundamental meaning of the parable.

It is by seeking out the fundamental assertion that we discern the intention of the sacred author. This is how Vatican II puts it:

'Those who seek out the intention of the sacred writers must, among other things, have regard for 'literary forms'. For truth is proposed and expressed in a variety of ways, depending on whether a text is a history of one kind or another, or whether its form is that of prophecy, poetry, or some other type of speech. The interpreter must investigate what meaning the sacred writer intended to express and actually expressed in particular circumstances as he used contemporary literary forms in accordance with the situation of his own time and culture. For the correct understanding of what the author wanted to assert, due attention must be paid to the customary and characteristic styles of perceiving, speaking, and narrating which prevailed at the time of the sacred writer, and to the customs men followed at that period in their everyday dealings with one another.' *(DV 12)*

To be able to distinguish the different literary forms used in the Bible, and thereby to identify the fundamental assertions the Bible makes, is probably the single most important quality we need in this process of making the meaning of God's Word accessible to the people of our day. Fortunately, it is not so difficult as it may seem at first. 'Literary forms' are used not only by the authors of sacred scripture, but they are a feature of *all* human language. In other words, we use literary forms in our every day life — we have learned to use our own language complete with its literary forms from absorption of the culture in which we live. We interpret them spontaneously when other people use them in conversation with us; we use them naturally when trying to convey certain experiences. As far as concerns the written word, we do not expect, for example, the same kind of information from a railway time-table as from a collection of poems. We have become sensitive to the fundamental assertions of our literary units in our everyday way of speaking and writing, quite simply by our familiarity with it. The same is true of the Bible and its fundamental assertions: with increasing familiarity we will soon find it is not difficult to discern very readily what an author is trying to say, and what he does not say. Of course, you can help yourself considerably by working from an edition of the Bible with reliable notes and references. For example, a footnote in the standard edition of the *Jerusalem Bible* advises that *Luke 16:19-31* is a 'Parable in story form without reference to any historical personage'. However, commentaries, no matter how good, are no substitute for familiarity with scripture itself: scripture is its own best commentary.

3. *THEOLOGY OF REVELATION*

OUTDATED MODEL OF REVELATION

Theology, too, has contributed to the advances in how we understand meaning. Within theology, there has been a significant shift in the emphasis of what we mean by 'revelation'. The theology of revelation used to be defined as being concerned with 'how God spoke to man'. It looked on revelation as a past event: God spoke in the Old Testament through the Law, and the Prophets; God spoke in the New Testament through his Son, Christ Jesus. Through this revelation God informed man about certain truths, and these truths were, it was thought, contained in the words of scripture. Such a model of revelation might be characterised as having three stages:

a. God's actual revelation — as an event in the past;
b. the conservation of these revealed truths in scripture — the text of scripture is preserved and handed down by the Church;
c. the understanding of that revelation and response in faith on the part of the person who reads scripture — subjective acceptance of scripture.

REVELATION IS DYNAMIC

Such a model of revelation is inadequate, for several reasons. Firstly, because revelation is not merely about 'how God spoke to man' but rather about 'how God **speaks** to man'. Revelation is not a past and static event; it is a dynamic living act here and now. God's speaking to humankind will always have to make use of human words, because we, as human beings depend on words for the communication of meaning. But the words are purely a channel, an occasion, an external sacrament of what God is trying to do when he speaks to us. Similarly, our response in faith is not to the words themselves, but to the one who speaks them, to God.

The Second Vatican Council asks us to see revelation as a dynamic, ongoing process. In its document on revelation it begins by making its own the words of St John, which are very much in the present tense:

'We announce to you the eternal life which was with the Father, and has appeared to us . . .'

(DV 1, quoting 1 Jn 1:2-3)

It sees the purpose of the Church itself as being to keep alive God's revelation:

'Christ the Lord . . . commissioned the apostles to preach the gospel . . . This commission was faithfully fulfilled by the apostles who, by their oral preaching, by example, and by ordinances, handed on what they had received from the lips of Christ, from living with him, and from what he did, or what they had learned through the prompting of the Holy Spirit. The commission was fulfilled, too, by those apostles and apostolic men who under the inspiration of the same Holy Spirit committed the message of salvation to writing.

But in order **to keep the gospel forever whole and alive** within the Church, the apostles left bishops as their successors . . .

And so the apostolic preaching, which is expressed in a special way in the inspired books, **was to be preserved** by a continuous succession of preachers **until the end of time** . . .

This tradition which comes from the apostles develops in the Church with the help of the Holy Spirit. For **there is a growth in the understanding of the realities and the words which have been handed down.** This happens through the contemplation and study made by believers, who treasure these things in their hearts *(cf. Lk 2:19 & 51)* . . .

. . . as the centuries succeed one another, **the Church constantly moves forward towards the fullness of divine truth until the words of God reach their complete fulfillment in her.**

Through the same tradition . . . **the sacred writings are more profoundly understood and unceasingly made active in her; and thus God, who spoke of old, uninterruptedly converses with the Bride of his beloved Son**; and the Holy Spirit, through whom the living voice of the gospel resounds in the Church, and through her, in the world, leads unto all truth those who believe and makes the word of Christ dwell abundantly in them *(cf. Col 3:16).' (DV 7-8)*

That rather long quote is typical of the whole of the document: it is pervaded by a strong sense that God's revelation is not merely a distant historical event in the past, but that it continues, and will go on until the end of time, when all will be revealed in a final way.

This very dynamic theology of revelation has two very important consequences for us as we struggle to discern the meaning of scripture: first of all, it brings God much closer to us here and now as we read and study his word. In other words, God is not far removed from us somewhere at the first stage of revelation, while we find ourselves at the third;

secondly, because it is a dynamic process, it depends on us. Revelation is not some kind of parcel that we have to unpack to discover the truth. Revelation is God's invitation to the Church to delve ever more deeply into the mystery of salvation.

'... the Church is concerned to move ahead daily towards a deeper understanding of the sacred scriptures' *(DV 23)*.

'This happens through the contemplation and study made by believers, who treasure these things in their hearts *(cf. Lk 2:19 & 5 & 51). (DV 8)*

This is the great paradox of revelation: that it is God's initiative, and his alone; yet he has chosen to depend on us and our human understanding. St John Chrysostom referred to it as God's 'condescension' — and Vatican II echoed him:

'In sacred scripture, while the truth and holiness of God always remain intact, the marvellous condescension of eternal wisdom is clearly shown 'that we may learn the gentle kindness of God, which words cannot express, and how far he has gone in adapting his language with thoughtful concern for our weak human nature.' For the words of God, expressed in human language, have been made like human discourse, just as of old the Word of the eternal Father, when he took to himself the weak flesh of humanity, became like other men.' *(DV 13, quoting John Chrysostom's 'On Genesis' 3:8)*

REVELATION IS OF GOD

The second reason that the static view of revelation is inadequate is that it objectifies the content of revelation: it presents scripture as containing certain truths which are necessary for us to know to achieve salvation. Yes, there is a real sense in which scripture is the source for our knowledge of certain dogmatic truths, but essentially **God does not reveal truths, he reveals himself**. Again, this is made unambiguously clear by Vatican II:

'In his goodness and wisdom, **God chose to reveal himself** and to make known to us the hidden purpose of his will *(cf. Eph 1:9)* by which through Christ, the Word made flesh, man has access to the Father in the Holy Spirit and comes to share in the divine nature *(cf. Eph 2:18 & 2 Pet 1:4)*. Through this revelation, therefore the invisible God *(cf. Col 1:15; 1 Tim 1:17)* out of the abundance of his love speaks to men as friends *(cf. Ex 33:11; Jn 15:14-15)* and lives among them *(cf. Bar 3:38)* so that he may invite and take them into fellowship with himself . . .' *(DV 2)* **'Through divine revelation, God chose to show forth and communicate himself** and the eternal decisions of his will regarding the salvation of men.' *(DV 6)* Through revelation God makes himself known to us. What we learn through revelation is not an abstract truth, but an experience of God himself. When God introduces himself, he will obviously communicate some truths about himself. Truths, therefore, will be an accompaniment, a consequence, a necessary ingredient, of the revelation of God. But God's word cannot be identified solely with those truths. God's revelation is a meeting, or at least an invitation to a meeting, between God and man. It is a dynamic event, not a static acceptance of truths. It is not the communication of abstract notions, but the communication of God himself, who is life.

CONCLUSION

The mistake in the old theological concept of revelation, then, lay in granting too much importance to the words themselves. When God speaks to humankind, he employs human words. God speaking to us actually makes use of the words of scripture. This is true whether we consider people at the time of Christ or in the Church today. God makes use of the words as they have been handed down (literally, 'tradition') by the Church, that is, in the actual scriptures we possess. But the over-riding, eminently important and absolutely vital element in revelation is that we see it as the self-revelation of God himself. The words are only the occasion, the external symbol or sacrament, the lasting visible memorial of an event that is ever new. What matters in any and every part of scripture is the contact with the living God himself. The experience of God to which the biblical authors bear witness ought to spark off in ourselves the living experience of God in our situation here and now. That is what revelation is about. The real meaning of the Bible, therefore, is not in the correct communication of abstract truths, but in bringing about this new, live experience of God in our own days.

THE KEY MESSAGE

In order to do justice to the passage we are reading, we ourselves should first have a good idea of its overall message. We have referred to this earlier as the 'fundamental assertion' of the passage (cf. pp. 60f.). It amounts to the main teaching the inspired author wanted to convey through this particular unit of writing. Once we are clear ourselves on what the fundamental assertion is we can then think of our particular community, and try to formulate the fundamental assertion in the most appropriate way. This we call the **'key message'.**

The single most useful tool in helping any scripture passage to proclaim its message is a clear announcement of the key message before the passage itself is read. It focuses everyone's attention on the central point of the passage. It serves as a guide to the people in sifting the information by announcing what is relevant, and what is not. People need such help: indeed, they get such help in every other sphere of communication — the essential contents of a newspaper report are announced by the headline or caption; in news broadcasting on radio and television, the news stories are headlined before being dealt with in detail. People are bombarded with a complex mass of communication which is often consequently confused or ignored. A key message given before the actual text eliminates vagueness and ambiguity.

The key message is not the scriptural reference. Such a reference has its own significance and relevance, but since it does not tell us anything about the meaning of the text, it does not constitute the key message.

The key message is not a summary of the text. It does not try to cover all the details of the text or enumerate its various elements, or even to recapitulate all its main points. The key statement limits itself to the overall teaching of the whole passage for a particular community.

It would also be wrong to identify the key message with a striking section of the passage. The Lectionary does seem to provide a sort of 'title' for the scripture passages, which are always a striking phrase lifted from within the reading. The exact purpose of this catch phrase is not at all clear, but it is certainly other than the point of the key message, which is to encapsulate the central message. For example, the 2nd Sunday of Lent always has the gospel of the transfiguration. In the Lectionary, the titling phrases are:

Year A — 'His face shone like the sun'
Year B — 'This is my Son, the Beloved'
Year C — 'As Jesus prayed, the aspect of his face was changed'

Do any of these capture the essential point of the Gospel episode? Even in they did, do they present it in a way which seems relevant to your community? No; it needs something simpler, and more direct, along the lines of 'Jesus gives a glimpse of his true self'.

My experience in formulating key messages and in checking those formulated by others has led me to draw up the following guidelines. Use it to evaluate your key messages.

Ideally, a key message should:
1. be a statement or an exhortation
   (it should be formulated as a complete sentence; anything less complete is less effective);
2. be short;
3. express the main teaching
   (what we have called the 'fundamental assertion' of the passage);
4. be worded in everyday language
   (it should not contain unusual biblical phrases or anything that reduces the directness of the statement);
5. be meaningful to the audience (and the occasion);
6. address your community directly
   (it should not be phrased in too general terms; it should normally include 'we' or 'you').

In other words, the key message should be formulated in a language relevant to our own situation and day. We should keep out all scriptural or theological jargon. We have to tell our community bluntly, in their own everyday language, what the particular text means to them.

Since scripture is basically an event in which God here and now communicates himself, the key message must reflect this aspect of encounter here and now. It should not present the message of scripture in third person terms. Through scripture God is speaking to me, to us, now — and the key message must capture that. The aspect of God's revelation as an encounter here and now must be assured. The key message for the Epiphany Gospel (Matthew 2:1-12) is not 'Wise men visit the infant Jesus', or still worse 'The visit of the wise men'. The text is not recounting a neutral event of past history; it is making a demand on our own attitude to Christ. The key message must express this: 'We should recognise and worship Jesus as universal King, like the Wise Men did'.

The formulation of the 'key message' is very literally part of the ministry of the Word. As readers we are called to serve the Word of God. That Word of God is presented to us in a fixed written form, a text written by an inspired author. Whatever else 'inspiration' means, it implies that the meaning God intended the text to have is what the author wants to teach by it. This is what is meant by the 'fundamental assertion'. This fundamental assertion is therefore objective; it is given by God through the text, and does not depend on the interpretation of the reader.

However, since the message has to be translated to living persons and to everyday life, there will be individual ways in which the fundamental assertion is experienced as the 'key message' by different readers. For example, *Genesis 12:1-4* contains God's invitation to Abraham: 'Come, be my people'. As such, the fundamental assertion is the same for all. However, the text occurs twice in the Lectionary:
— 2nd Lent, Year A. In the baptismal context of Lent, especially if the catechumenate is being celebrated, it can have the key message of highlighting the intimate relationship with himself that God initiates through the sacrament; alternatively, in the penitential context, it might by expressed in an invitation to return to that relationship.
— religious profession. In such a context it may refer rather to God's free choosing, and his promise of lasting support.

What do you think about the following 'key messages'?

—Ezekiel 37: 1-14 (Vigil of Pentecost; 5th Lent C);
   the vision of dry bones; city parish congregation;
   suggested key message:
   'However much we may be dead spiritually through our sins and shortcomings, God can restore us to life again.'
—Ecclesiaticus 27: 16-21;
   on friendship; secondary school audience;
   suggested key message:
   'If a friend tells you a secret, do not betray their trust. Do not discuss this secret with others.'
—2 Kings 19:15-19
   Hezekiah's prayer; a community of religious sisters;
   suggested key message:
   'We should bring our problems to the presence of God in the Blessed Sacrament. God will console us.'
—Matthew 14:1-12;
   John the Baptist's death; college/university students;
   suggested key message:
   'Murder is murder; sin is sin — even if it happens at a birthday party.'

—Hebrews 5:1-10;
  Christ's priesthood; for seminarians;
  suggested key message:
  'If you want to become a priest, you must be humble and self-sacrificing as Jesus was.'

DECODING

Even if we are making use of a reasonable translation, it may be that we come across words or constructions whose meaning will not be immediately obvious to the particular audience for whom we are reading. Since it is the reader's task to convey the meaning of the text as accurately as possible, it may mean having to decode the words or constructions in question.

When we speak we are expressing an experience in words. In fact, we are converting that experience into units of sound which are sent by vibrations in the air to someone else's ears. Let us call the process by which we verbalise our experience **'encoding'**. The sounds, as it were, are **the code** in which we have wrapped the message. The sound strikes the ears of the recipient, whence it is relayed by little nerves to his brain. The listener then has to **decode** the message, that is to say, analyse the sounds and establish their meaning.

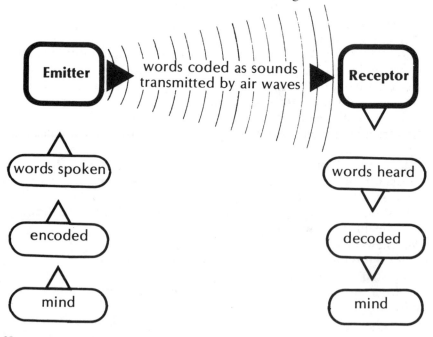

This is only a simple model to illustrate the principle of the transmission of the spoken word. The process of encoding and decoding is very complicated. The human brain is capable of decoding an enormous amount of information from a great deal of sound in a very short time. The capacity to decode varies from individual to individual depending on a whole variety of factors, but perhaps principally on the culture and milieu in which that individual habitually operates. Obviously, for example, different categories of professions are adept at decoding the set of vocabulary and jargon connected with that profession: thus medical terminology will be commonplace for doctors nurses, while engineers have their specialised vocabulary.

The problem for us as readers is that we are faced not with an individual, but with an audience of listeners. Fortunately, we share more in common in our decoding ability than differences because of specialisation, but we do need to remember that whether the message reaches our hearers depends directly on

A. the code itself — are they able to decode it?

B. the transmission of the code — is there any extraneous interference?

A. HINDRANCES TO DECODING

A prime duty when preparing for reading is to know, as far as possible, the decoding ability of the audience for whom we are reading. This is something that can only be learned by experience. One obvious way to verify is by asking the members of your community if they felt they benefited from your reading. In particular you might ask:

Did you get the message?

Was the meaning clear?

You may be surprised to see how honest answers can lead you to better reading in future.

This kind of feedback is essential — remember, too, that the whole audience may be giving you a more subtle feedback in the way they actually receive the reading (cf. body language, pp.42f).

The main hindrances to decoding fall into four categories:

a. unknown words that need decoded

b. the context needs decoded

c. difficult grammatical constructions need decoded

d. unfamiliar cultural customs need decoded

a. Unknown words

Certain words may need to be decoded because they are not part of the audience's habitual vocabulary. For example, in this sentence 'The chief priests and the whole Sanhedrin were looking for evidence against Jesus, however false . . .' *(Mt 26:59 & Mk 14:55 JB)*, the word 'Sanhedrin' may need to be decoded for the hearers as 'the supreme council'.

Certain words may need to be decoded, not because they are inherently difficult, but because they are not specific enough. For example, in Matthew 9:18 we read:

'While he was speaking to them, up came one of the officials,
who bowed low in front of him . . .' *(JB)*

The unspecified pronouns make it impossible to tell who is speaking to whom; and one of which officials came up to him? For any normal audience this ought to be simply decoded as:

'While Jesus was speaking to the disciples of John the Baptist, up came one of the officials from the synagogue who . . .'

Certain words may need decoded because although they seem to be familiar to the audience, in fact their meaning in the scriptural text has different nuances. For example, supposing we have to read *Ecclesiastes 1:2; 2:21-23* (First reading, 18th Ordinary Sunday, Year C):

'Vanity of vanities, the Preacher says. Vanity of vanities. All is vanity!

For so it is that a man who has laboured wisely, skilfully and successfully must leave what is his own to someone who has not toiled for it at all. This, too, is vanity and great injustice; for what does he gain for all the toil and strain that he has undergone under the sun? What of all his laborious days, his cares of office, his restless nights? This, too, is vanity.' *(JB)*

This text has an important message. Not only this reading, but the whole of the Book of Ecclesiastes, hinges on the word 'vanity'. Ordinarily, we take 'vanity' to refer to a character trait: it implies self-praise, smugness, conceit, a certain amount of ostentation. Unfortunately, this is not the meaning of 'vanity' in the text. Our English expression 'in vain' is closer to the meaning of the original Hebrew. הבל hebel

'. . . means primarily mist, breath, one of the traditional group of images (water, shadow, smoke, etc.) used in Hebrew poetry to describe the transitory nature of man. But in Ecclesiastes that word has lost this sense and signifies only the illusory nature of things and hence the delusions to which they subject mankind.' *(JB footnote to Ecclesiastes 1c.)*

The inspired writer is trying to get across to us the pointlessness and futility of human life. Unless we decode 'vanity' we run the serious risk of allowing our hearers to miss the message. There are two ways in which 'vanity' might be decoded: it might be possible to have a brief explanation before we start reading the text itself (cf. simple guided reading, pp. 81f); or we may substitute another expression for 'vanity' — for example, we might read it as:

> 'Utterly useless, the Preacher says. Utterly useless. All is pointless and in vain . . .'

b. the context

The way texts have been chosen for inclusion in the Lectionary most often follows the natural shape of the original scripture passage. That is to say, certain natural units can be detected within scripture, and in the main these have been followed in where a Lectionary text begins and where it ends. Sometimes, though, the natural scripture unit may be too large to be a single Lectionary text, and it may be spread over two or more Sundays. For example, in his Gospel Matthew gathers the sayings of Jesus together, and presents them as five great sermons. Let us consider the most famous of these, which is most often known as 'the sermon on the mount'. In Matthew's Gospel this occupies the whole of chapters 5, 6 and 7. The Lectionary's use of this total unit is spread over six Sundays (4th to 9th Ordinary Sundays, Year A). Obviously, within the total unit, there are smaller, self-contained sections, and it is these that the Lectionary presents. Whereas Matthew only has to set the context once, the Lectionary has to do it six times. Notice how the Lectionary itself supplements the Gospel text in the latter five weeks by prefacing it with the simple context: 'Jesus said to his disciples: . . .'. Instead of an anonymous passage it is now clear who is speaking and to whom his message is addressed.

There are times when, for good pastoral reasons, our choice of text is not from the Lectionary: on such occasions we should imitate the way the Lectionary supplies whatever context is needed for us to grasp the message of what follows.

We should equally be prepared to supplement the context the Lectionary provides if we feel that it needs further decoding for our particular community. In the example we have just discussed, the 'sermon on the mount', Matthew himself set the context the way he did for a clear and specific purpose: he was concerned to present Jesus as

71

the new Moses, who had come to replace the Old Covenant and its Law by the New Covenant and its Law of Love. Consequently he deliberately portrays Jesus as going up the hill to speak to the people, parallel to Moses ascent of Mount Sinai to receive the Law *(Ex 24:12-18)*. This context was important to Matthew because he is addressing his Gospel in the first place to people from a Jewish background: he is setting Jesus in a context whose symbolism would help clarify the import and nature of the message which follows. We may feel that the evangelist's deliberate choice of context is useful for our understanding of the text, and therefore we need to make sure that the context is made clear. Again, there are several ways this might be achieved: through explanation in the homily; through a brief explanation before reading the actual text; by repeating Matthew's setting of the context in each of the subsequent weeks, thus:

'Seeing the crowds, Jesus had gone up the hill. There he had sat down and had been joined by his disciples. Then he had begun to speak. This is what he taught them: . . .'

c. decoding difficult constructions

Earlier we drew a simple model of how encoding and decoding operates. In fact, when decoding, we make use of what is called 'immediate memory'. That is to say, we do not decode individual sounds, but store the information they give us until they compose a complete unit, and then decode that to discover the meaning of the unit.

For example,
will not all subordinate clauses,
of which there may be several,
some adjectival,
some adverbial,
some more intricate than others,
be suspended in our understanding
until the sentence is complete?
Once the whole unit is complete we push the whole sentence away to make room for the next flow of information.

The capacity of this 'immediate memory' varies from person to person, depending on practice and study. Children and uneducated persons can usually store no more than short sentences and the simplest of constructions. Beyond that, the 'immediate memory' becomes too full, and the message starts to be lost.

Schematically, the capacity of 'immediate memory' can be represented like this:

	primary	secondary	academic
average words per sentence	10	15	20
maximum words per sentence	20	30	40
maximum level of subordination	3	5	7

Over and above, there are several 'complicating factors':

—*unusual sentence order*

e.g. 'Yesterday — much later than we expected — nobody less came than the bishop himself.'

—*length of sentences*

—*subordination of thoughts*

e.g. 'She is the daughter of the Nizam's favourite wife's personal physician.'

—*clauses*

—*complicated words*

e.g. 'ornithological species of great similarity invariably congregate in close proximity' instead of 'birds of a feather flock together'.

We need to be aware of the 'immediate memory' capacity of those to whom we are reading, and need to adapt the way we read accordingly. For example, let us take *Ephesians 1:3ff.* (Second reading, 15th Ordinary Sunday, Year B). The text begins:

'Blessed be God the Father of our Lord Jesus Christ,
who has blessed us with all the spiritual blessings of heaven
in Christ.
Before the world was made, he chose us, chose us in Christ,
to be holy and spotless, and to live through love in his
presence,
determining that we should become his adopted sons,
through Jesus Christ
for his own kind purposes,
to make us praise the glory of his grace,
his free gift to us in the Beloved,
in whom, through his blood, we gain our freedom, the
forgiveness of our sins . . .

Even for a well trained mind, it is difficult enough to follow the long and complicated construction of the text when it is clearly before us in written form. Even then it takes time to analyse which clauses qualify which others. There are very few people whose 'immediate memory' would be capable of storing the second sentence in the text; it has too many thought units, each of which has to fall into its proper place. After ten words, if not sooner, the average listener will surrender to a feeling of general incomprehension.

A good reader will decode the text for his hearers by removing the complicating factors: in our example from Ephesians that means breaking the long sentence with its subordinate clauses and involved cross references down into smaller sentences. So that it becomes clear which clause refers to whom or to what we will need to repeat the key words or phrases in the smaller sentences: such repetition is known as 'purposeful redundancy'. The Ephesians text then might be read as:

'Blessed be God the Father of our Lord Jesus Christ,
who has blessed us with all the spiritual blessings of heaven
in Christ.

Before the world was made, *God* chose us,
he chose us in Christ.
God chose us to be holy and spotless,
and to live through love in his presence.
Before the world was made
God determined that we should become his adopted sons,
through Jesus Christ.
God determined to do this for his own kind purposes,
to make us praise the glory of his grace;
that grace which is his free gift to us in *Christ*, his Beloved
Son.

It is in Christ, through his blood, *that* we gain our freedom,
that we gain the forgiveness of our sins . . .'

The phrases in italics are those that have been repeated for purposeful redundancy.

d. unfamiliar cultural customs

All cultures develop their own customs, symbolic ways of doing things, gestures which have a special significance. It is natural, then, that the texts of scripture, should reflect the times and the culture in which their authors wrote them. Some of the customs that are alluded to in the Bible are readily understood, but there are others that need to be decoded.

The cultural customs that we are liable to find in the Bible may need decoded for one of two reasons:

—the text may straightforwardly refer to some custom which we feel is unfamiliar to our hearers, and we will need to help them decode its significance. In fact, the Gospel writers themselves often provide examples of decoding customs that they thought would be unfamiliar to their readers. So, for example, Mark, writing for the church at Rome most probably, feels he has to explain the Jewish purification customs to his non-Jewish readers:

> 'The Pharisees and some of the scribes who had come from Jerusalem gathered round Jesus, and they noticed that some of his disciples were eating with unclean hands, *that is, without washing them. For the Pharisees, and the Jews in general, follow the traditions of the elders and never eat without washing their arms as far as the elbow; and on returning from the market place they never eat without first sprinkling themselves. There are also many other observances which have been handed down to them concerning the washing of cups and pots and bronze dishes.* So these Pharisees and scribes . . .' *(Mk 7:1-5 JB)*

The section in italics shows Mark decoding the purification customs for us, so that we will be able to appreciate the point of the controversy which is to follow. This is perhaps the longest and clearest example, but there are many other smaller ones. In John's Gospel we find:

> '. . . Jesus said to the Samaritan woman, 'Give me a drink' . .
> . . . The Samaritan woman said to him, 'What? You are a Jew and you ask me, a Samaritan for a drink?' — *Jews, in fact, do not associate with Samaritans.* Jesus replied . . . *(Jn 4:9 JB)*.

Again, John's decoding is clearly indicated in italics. The interesting thing about this particular example is that Luke, writing above all for Greek converts often uses a token Samaritan in his Gospel, precisely because they were despised by the Jews, and regarded as foreigners — and Luke's Samaritans are always portrayed in a good light. The classical example is the parable of the Good Samaritan, who proves himself more sensitive to the demands of charity than the Jewish priest and the Levite *(Lk 10:29-37)*. Another example is the cure of the ten lepers:

> '. . . Finding himself cured, one of them turned back praising God at the top of his voice and threw himself at the feet of Jesus and thanked him. The man was a Samaritan . . .' *(Lk 17:11-19 JB)*

That final phrase was very significant for the converts at Antioch for whom Luke first wrote his Gospel, but is that significance transparent enough for us today? Should we not literally copy John the evangelist, and add 'Jews, in fact, do not associate with Samaritans'?

—a second way in which a custom may need to be decoded is more subtle. The custom may be implicit in the biblical description or episode, and at first sight there may not seem to be anything that has to be decoded. In fact, however, if we are to draw the full meaning from the text, that custom has to be made explicit by decoding.

The commonest example of this is where the Gospels depict Jesus as saying or doing something at some particular Jewish feast: the full significance of Jesus' words or actions comes across only when we decode what that feast meant for the Jews.

You will find that you soon become familiar with the basic customs referred to in scripture, and as you become more proficient you will be able to discern and appreciate deeper levels which you can then decode for your hearers. Here is a particularly subtle example, which is the 'tribute to Caesar' dispute: the episode is presented by all three synoptics as during the last days of Jesus' life (Mark makes it the Tuesday before Jesus' death), and it takes place within the precincts of the Temple itself. The Pharisees and some Herodians approach Jesus and ask 'Is it permissible to pay taxes to Caesar or not?' Their question was a trick one: if Jesus answers positively, he will be seen as supporting the oppressive Roman occupation; if negatively, he can be branded as a rebel. Instead of answering directly, Jesus asks to see a coin. They produce a denarius. 'Whose head is this? Whose name?' Jesus asks. 'Caesar's' they replied. He then said to them, 'Very well, give back to Caesar what belongs to Caesar — and to God what belongs to God.'

All three synoptics add a footnote which seems to suggest Jesus' answer devastated his oponents:

Matthew: 'This reply took them by surprise, and they left him alone and went away.' *(22:22 JB)*

Mark: 'This reply took them completely by surprise.' *(12:17b JB)*

Luke: 'As a result, they were unable to find fault with anything he had to say in public; his answer took them by surprise and they were silenced.' *(20:26 JB)*

On the face of it, Jesus seemed to have side-stepped the question rather than to have answered it so decisively. The force of Jesus' reply comes from Jewish custom implicit in the episode.

Remember that (two) days earlier Jesus expelled the money-changers from the Temple: they had been there to conduct a legitimate and necessary business. Necessary because Jewish ritual custom and law prescribed that only the official Temple coinage was legal tender within the Temple precincts. The reason underlying this was that foreign coinage, Roman in particular, was minted with the head of the emperor as god: such coins represented a graven image of a false god, a direct contravention of the first commandment.

Returning to the episode aware of the custom, we see that Jesus' opponents who come to him with a trick question, are themselves caught out, not so much by Jesus' final reply, but because they are caught red-handed in a symbolic contravention of the first and greatest commandment.

This particular example may require so much decoding that it could not be done by inserting a phrase within the reading itself; the meaning would probably be better served if a brief explanation preceded the actual reading.

B. EXTRANEOUS INTERFERENCE

The message may be endangered, not by any fault in the coding itself, but because of extraneous interference.

Have you ever tried to keep up a conversation in a railway compartment while the train is passing through a tunnel? You probably had to give up very soon because of the deafening noise surrounding you.

Returning to our model, the transmission between emitter and receptor is by means of sound waves. If those speaking sounds are blurred by other noise, proper understanding becomes difficult, if not impossible. Technically speaking, everything that interferes with the reception of sound is known as 'noise'.

'Noise' can be of two types: external or interior.

When we come to read in church, there is much more external noise than we might at first think. As a little experiment, try sitting with your eyes closed and listen specifically for the external noise: benches creak; people cough; babies gurgle, cry, or even scream; insects buzz; people drop money, drop books; traffic noise; etc.

On top of that we must also reckon with interior noise, which is whatever interferes with the reception of the sound in the mind of the hearer. Such interior noise is made up by the distractions of everyday living: the need to shift position on a hard bench, or to stretch a leg; preoccupation with something that has to be done worries of one kind or another; tiredness.

In fact, nobody actually hears the full flow of sound produced by a reader. Normally we hear only in patches, with parts blurred or blotted out by interfering 'noise'.

Fortunately human language has devised a way if not of preventing this loss, then of compensating for it. Quite simply, it depends on the more important parts of human discourse being repeated sufficiently to compensate for losses caused by noise. Such repetition is known as *'redundance'*. In a written literary work, redundance might by frowned on, but in oral communication it becomes indispensable. When used in such a context, we refer to it as *'purposeful redundancy'*.

The essence of 'purposeful redundancy' lies in repetition. However, there are different forms of repetition, and they are not to be used indiscriminately:

— explicit repetition when a whole phrase is repeated;
— implicit or mutual repetition when repetition is contained in the use of parallel words or phrases.

By skilfull mixing of the forms of repetition a message can become so redundant that it can be received and understood even against a very heavy background of noise. A railway station is usually a noisy place, so effective announcements will depend on good use of purposeful redundance:

'This is an announcement for passengers travelling to Glasgow. Passengers travelling to Glasgow should proceed to platform 12. I repeat: the train for passengers travelling to Glasgow is at platform 12.'

Not all the elements in a message are of equal importance. The message hinges on a few key words that are essential. These are the words that need to be repeated if we want to make the message sufficiently redundant. In the station announcement the key words are 'Glasgow' and 'platform 12'.

When reading a passage from the Bible we may not be competing with a station-size din, but we should reckon on a good amount of noise. Our reading should be made sufficiently redundant to offset this interference. We will see in more detail in the following section how to do this in practice, but it involves, for example, highlighting the key message and announcing it before reading the actual text itself; recognising key words or key phrases and reading these with special care and emphasis, or even repeating them; substituting pronouns by the appropriate key nouns.

THE PREPARATION AND READING OF THE TEXT

What is said in this section presumes all of what has gone before: what follows represents the practical drawing together of the many strands.

PREPARATION

We should never presume to read without proper preparation. The practice, all too common, of thrusting the text of a reading on someone at the last minute is deplorable. No person, however competent a public reader, can do justice to the text without dedicating a considerable amount of time to preparing how it is to be read.

In practice, preparation ought to consist of five stages:

1. Reading the text to determine **the key message**
2. Reading the text to identify words, phrases etc. that need to be **decoded**
3. Reading the text with an eye to **purposeful redundancy**
4. Reading the text to plan **voice modulation** and use of **pauses**
5. Arranging the reading in the form of a **specific technique**

Perfect preparation requires that at the end we read the text aloud precisely as we plan to read it in the actual liturgical celebration.

This analysis of the text and the process of preparation will gradually take less time as we become more adept, more expert at the art of liturgical reading. At first it will probably be necessary to plan out our pattern of reading in writing; later we may be able to prepare ourselves without any such need to write anything down, noting in our memory how we have planned to present the reading.

1. Reading the text so as to formulate *the key message*

See the section on the Key message, pp. 65ff.

2. Reading the text with a view to *decoding*

See the section on Decoding, pp. 68ff.

3. Reading the text with a view to adding *purposeful redundancy*

See the section on Redundancy, pp. 77f.; see also pp. 73-4.

4. Reading the text with a view to *voice modulation* and *pauses*

See the section on Voice regulation, pp. 38f.; and on Pauses, pp. 40f.

5. Reading the text with a view to using a *specific reading technique*

See the section on Specific techniques, pp. 81ff.

5. SPECIFIC TECHNIQUES

A. SIMPLE GUIDED READING

The technique we call 'simple guided reading' is one way of presenting a reading as clearly and effectively as possible. It is called 'simple' because it involves minimal interference with the text itself; instead the emphasis in this technique is in having a very brief introduction before the reading of the actual text.

Schematically, the technique can be represented as:

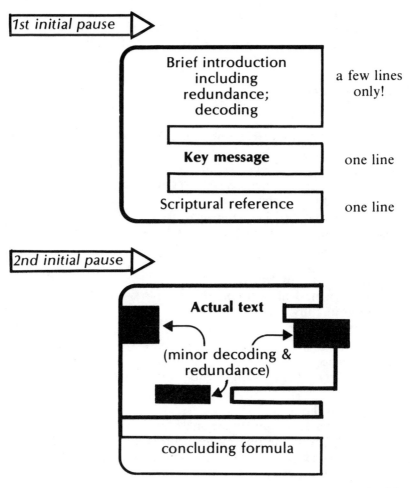

Most, if not all, the *decoding* is done in the introduction. However, where minor changes in the text itself are possible, this is to be preferred (keep the introduction as brief as possible)

The same applies to *redundance.* It may be necessary to read a key sentence twice.

The *key message* focuses attention on the fundamental assertion, including the present relevance for the particular community. It may **never** be omitted (whereas the introduction may sometimes be superfluous for a highly trained audience)

The *scriptural reference* helps to divide off and distinguish the reader's own words from the scripture text itself.

This transition to the word of God is further indicated by the *second initial pause.*

Any *minor modifications* that we include within the reading of the text should be merely explicitations of what is already there.

FIRST EXAMPLE

The text:
Proverbs 9:1-6 (First Reading, 20th Ordinary Sunday, Year B)
'Wisdom has built herself a house,
she has erected her seven pillars,
she has slaughtered her beasts, prepared her wine,
she has laid her table.
She has despatched her maidservants
and proclaimed from the city's heights:
'Who is ignorant? Let him step this way.'
To the fool she says,
'Come and eat my bread,
drink the wine I have prepared!
Leave your folly and you will live,
walk in the ways of perception.' *(JB)*

The audience:
An ordinary, average congregation; principally adult.

Analysis of the text:
Fundamental assertion: Everyone is invited to learn God's wisdom.
Details (i.e. how the text builds up this assertion): in this example,
it is by extended metaphor, where each image contributes to the
overall message:—

82

—learning wisdom is like taking part in a festive meal;
—the maidservants stand for those who help us to learn wisdom, teachers, etc.;
—the bread and wine stand for the truths of wisdom that we are to learn.

Decoding:
—'Wisdom' = the knowledge of how to please God,
the knowledge of how to live our lives so as to please God in this world, so as to be happy with him in the next; 'Wisdom' is personified;
—'seven pillars' = (probably) the perfect setting for entertaining guests;
—'ignorant' = the person who lacks wisdom, experience of life;
—'fool' & 'folly' = refer to people who are uneducated, uninstructed.

More decoding may be necessary of some of the customs alluded to: for example, 'slaughtering beasts', perhaps even the very idea of a banquet, etc.

Final form:

1st initial pause

'In many ways, we are ignorant and foolish:	Direct appeal
we are ignorant of the ways of God;	
we have no proper understanding of how we are to	
live to please God,	Decoding
of how to be truly happy in this life, and the next.	
To know this is to be truly wise.	
God, the supreme teacher of wisdom,	
or Wisdom itself,	
is like a queen who invites us to share in a feast.	To help the
That invitation comes through God's teachers,	personification of
presented here as the queen's maidservants.	Wisdom as a
Whoever accepts the invitation will enjoy God's	woman, we call
hospitality,	her 'queen'.
expressed in the images of a Jewish festive meal:	
(add whatever decoding of customs may be necessary)	Only the essential
The bread and wine offered to us all	minimum
are God's own words of teaching and instruction.	

	Key message
'Everyone of us is invited to share God's wisdom.'	
'A reading from the book of Proverbs.'	Scriptural reference
2nd initial pause	About four seconds
'Wisdom has built herself a house, *Wisdom* has erected her seven pillars,	Redundance: key word 'wisdom' repeated
DP:1	Dividing pause: one second
she has slaughtered her beasts, ↑ prepared her wine, she has laid her table.	
DP:1	Dividing pause: one second
↑↑*Wisdom* has despatched her maidservants and proclaimed from the city's heights:	Redundance heighten pitch to indicate climax
SP:1	Stress pause: one second
'Who is ignorant? Let him step this way.'	Slow to stress key message
DP:3	Dividing pause: three seconds
To the fool Wisdom says, ↓ 'Come and eat my bread, drink the wine I have prepared! ↓ Leave your folly,	Slow, with pauses, to stress meaning
SP:2	Stress pause: two seconds
and you will live,	
SP:2	Stress pause: two seconds

walk in the ways of perception.'

This is the Word of the Lord.

The text:
Jeremiah 38:4-6, 8-10 (First reading, 20th Ordinary Sunday, Year C)

The king's leading men spoke to the king. 'Let Jeremiah be put to death: he is unquestionably disheartening the remaining soldiers in the city, and all the people too, by talking like this. The fellow does not have the welfare of the people at heart so much as its ruin.' 'He is in your hands as you know,' King Zedekiah answered 'for the king is powerless against you.' So they took Jeremiah and threw him into the well of Prince Malchiah in the Court of the Guard, letting him down with ropes. There was no water in the well, only mud, and into the mud Jeremiah sank.

Ebed-melech came out from the city palace and spoke to the king, 'My lord king,' he said 'these men have done a wicked thing by treating the prophet Jeremiah like this: they have thrown him into the well where he will die.' At this the king gave Ebed-melech the Cushite the following order: 'Take three men with you from here and pull the prophet Jeremiah out of the well before he dies.'

Audience:
An ordinary, average parish congregation; principally adult.

Analysis of the text:
Fundamental assertion: God's Word must be proclaimed, in season and out.

Decoding: – *context:* the verses the Lectionary presents are extracts, albeit the crucial ones, from a larger event. We need to check the immediate context of Jeremiah 38, and even Jeremiah 36-38. We need to decode that Jeremiah is in prison because he has advised surrender to the Babylonian army which is besieging Jerusalem: he has prophesied the downfall of the city and the people as a punishment from God.

other details: 'Ebed-melech the Cushite' = an Ethiopian courtier serving in the king's palace.

Reading this larger context also reveals that the king was weak and easily swayed — convey this in the way we present the king's words.

Final form:

1st initial pause

Jerusalem has been under siege by the
      Babylonian army;
Jeremiah, the prophet, has warned that, as a
punishment for breaking their covenant with God,
the city and the people are doomed to defeat.
Jeremiah advises surrender. His prophecy has
already landed him in prison, but still Jeremiah
proclaims the Word of the Lord that Jerusalem
will fall, even when he is threatened with death.

Decoding context

Suggesting fundamental assertion

We must proclaim what we know to be God's Word —
whatever the consequences.

Key message

A reading from the prophet Jeremiah

Scriptural reference

2nd initial pause

The King's leading men spoke to the king.
'Let Jeremiah be put to death:
he is unquestionably disheartening the remaining
soldiers in the city,
and all the people too,
by talking like this *of the capture of the city*.
The fellow does not have the welfare of the people
at heart so much as its ruin.'

Emphatically: slow

Decoding context

Stress key words in contrast

DP:1

Dividing pause: one second

'*Jeremiah* is in your hands
as you know,'
King Zedekiah answered
'for *I* am powerless against you.'

Convey irony in voice modulation

DP:1

Dividing pause: one second

86

So the king's leading men took Jeremiah *out of prison* and thrĕw him into the well . . . in the Court of the Guard, letting him down with ropes.	Decoding context Omission of unnecessary and complicating detail
There was no water in the well, only mud, and into the mud Jeremiah sank.	Slow, stress 'mud'
DP:3	Dividing pause: three seconds
Ebed-melech, *an Ethiopian courtier who served in the palace,* came out and spoke to the king, 'My lord king,' he said, these men have done a wĭcked thing by treating the prophet Jeremiah like this: they have thrown him into the well where he will die.' At this the king gave Ebed-melech (. . .) the following order: 'Take three men with you from here and pull the prophet Jeremiah out of the well bĕfore he dies.'	Decoding Slow Omission of unnecessary detail
This is the Word of the Lord.	

B. COMMENTATED READING

Sometimes the text that has to be proclaimed is so involved, so replete with meaning that a simple reading of it will not do justice to its message. We may find that there is so much decoding that any introduction would risk overloading our hearers' immediate memory. The introduction would then become self-defeating, and the reading will remain as meaningless as ever.

We need some other technique through which the full meaning of the text can be brought out. 'Commentated reading' consists essentially in enlarging the text with little explanatory phrases that are introduced wherever they may be required.

Schematically, the technique can be represented as:

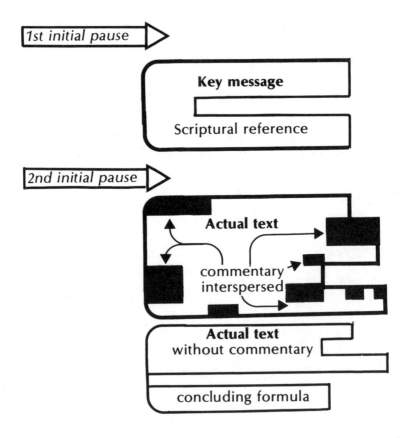

There is *no introduction* — any decoding whether of words or of context may be part of the commentary itself.

The *key message* is never omitted. It is essential to help the audience assimilate the meaning of the text for their own lives.

The *commentary* should flow with the actual text, and not along side it as an extra. The weight of the commentary will vary according to the needs of our community, and the amount of *decoding* that may be necessary. We must never forget, though, that the commentary must restrict itself to direct explanation of the text.

Wherever possible, we should read the *actual text* once more, this time without commentary. This has a twofold purpose: firstly, to make sure that the people hear clearly which is the text itself, and which is merely our commentary; secondly, it fulfills the function of purposeful redundance, giving the people one more opportunity to take in a difficult, but fruitful passage. It might be helpful to preface the second reading of the text by a statement such as: 'Let us hear the Word of God again, but now without commentary.' During this second reading we should follow the actual text without change (except for minor and indispensable modifications).

FIRST EXAMPLE

The text:
Proverbs 9:1-6 (First reading, 20th Ordinary Sunday, Year B) text as on page 82.

The audience:
Children, eight to twelve year-olds.

Analysis of the text:
This is essentially the same as before (pp. 82-3), but since we are dealing with children, even more decoding and redundance will be necessary.

Final form:

1st initial pause

Dear boys and girls,
God calls everyone of you to become wise,
to become holy.

Key message. Notice use of short constructions

This is what God tells us
in the book of Proverbs,
which I am going to read to you now.

2nd initial pause

Queen *Wisdom has built herself a house.*
God is telling us a little parable: we should
imagine that there is a very wise queen, a queen
who knows everything about God, and who can tell
us how we can be God's friends, and how we can
be holy. God says:
Queen *Wisdom has built herself a house.* And she has
prepared a special room for her guests, a beautiful
room with *seven pillars.*
More than that, she has prepared a wonderful party,
a great banquet: *she has slaughtered her beasts* so
that there will be enough fine meat for everyone;
she has prepared her wine, so that everybody will
have enough to drink; *she has laid the table*, so
that everything is ready for the guests.
Then Queen *Wisdom sent out her maidservants* to
invite her guests. The invitations were to go to
everyone who wanted to enjoy her goodness, so the
maids were told *to shout* the invitation from the
highest places in the city where everyone could
hear them.

DP:3

And what do you think the invitation was?

'Who is ignorant?;'
that means 'does any one want to learn about God?'
'Then *let him step this way.* Let him come to my party.
Anyone who wants to learn is welcome in my palace.
Nobody need feel left out.
You want to know about God?
Then come to my house and I will help you.'

DP:1

	Scripture reference
	About four seconds
	Literary form is explained
	Redundance
	Decoding 'banquet' customs
	Simplifying expressions
	Dividing pause: three seconds
	Key message: note how it is explained many times
	Dividing pause: one second

Yes, boys and girls, God says that Queen Wisdom
gives this invitation to anyone who feels *a fool*,
who feels they do not know enough about God,
and about what God wants them to do.
Queen Wisdom says:
'Come and eat my bread,
drink the wine I have prepared.'
Leave behind the way you do things,
being naughty, telling lies;
instead, come, and I will show you how to be good
and happy.'
That is what Queen Wisdom says.

Boys and girls, it is God that is talking to us here.
God himself is inviting us to come to him,
and to learn from him how to be wise,
how to live a life that is happy,
how to live a life that is holy.

Let us all listen again to the Words God
is speaking to us.
Let us listen carefully.
Because it has all been explained,
we ought to be able to understand it quite well
this time:

DP:2

'Wisdom has built herself a house.
Wisdom has set up a room with seven pillars.
She has slaughtered . . .'

(margin note: Simplifying expressions)

(margin note: Dividing pause: two seconds)

(margin note: Repeat text, with only minor modifications)

SECOND EXAMPLE

The text
Romans 5:12, 17-19 (Second Reading, 1st Lent, Year A: shortened
form)
    'Sin entered the world through one man, and through sin death,
and thus death has spread through the whole human race because
everyone has sinned. If it is certain that death reigned over everyone as

the consequence of one man's fall, it is even more certain that one man, Jesus Christ, will cause everyone to reign in life who receives the free gift that he does not deserve, of being made righteous. Again, as one man's fall brought condemnation on everyone, so the good act of one man brings everyone life and makes them justified. As by one man's disobedience many were made sinners, so by one man's obedience many will be made righteous.'

The audience:
The celebration of the liturgy of the Word for the rite of election, i.e. the admission of catechumens into the period of enlightenment, of final and intense preparation for the Easter sacraments. This is part of the christian initiation of adults; so we presume an adult congregation. Ideally, the rite should be celebrated in the course of the Sunday Mass.

Analysis of the text
Fundamental assertion: Everyone is made righteous, has new life, through Christ Jesus.
Details (i.e. how the text builds up this assertion):
 the meaning of the passage is constructed through a series of contrasts: death-life; condemned-righteous; disobedience-obedience; Adam (though never mentioned explicitly) — Jesus Christ. Those contrasts will be expressed most clearly by voice modulation.
Decoding: 'being made righteous' = being raised up (in contrast to 'fall'); or = being made holy (in contrast to 'sinners').
 Principally, though, decoding will mean simplifying the grammatical construction.

Final form:

1st initial pause	(As long as is necessary)
Jesus has delivered us from sin and death; he brings us to new life.	Key message
. In this season of Lent as we as we prepare to celebrate or to renew our baptism, the Church puts before us the inspired teaching of St Paul, from his letter to the Romans.	Scriptural reference

Saint Paul is contrasting Adam and Jesus:
more importantly, he is contrasting the consequences
of Adam's actions and Jesus' actions.
By natural birth we are sons and daughters of Adam;
by spiritual rebirth, that is, by baptism,
we are, like Christ, sons and daughters of God.
Through baptism,
what Paul speaks of happens in us.
Let us listen, then, to what St Paul tells us:

(Decoding literary form)

Direct appeal

2nd initial pause

About four seconds

Sin entered the world through one man, *Adam,*
and through sin death *entered the world,*
and thus death has spread through the whole
    human race,
because everyone has sinned.
As sons and daughters of Adam, we are
    condemned to die;
we are sinners.

First part of key message repeated

DP:3

Dividing pause: three seconds

If it is certain that death reigned over everyone
as the consequence of one man's fall,
it is even more certain that one man, Jesus Christ
will cause everyone to reign in life:
this new life is a free gift *of God,*
given through Jesus Christ,
given to us by God, given to all mankind,
though none of us deserve it.
By receiving this new life we are made righteous,

Note emphasis on key words of contrast

Simplified construction

Redundance

Second part of key message repeated

DP:3

Dividing pause: three seconds

Again,
as one man's fall brought condemnation on everyone,
so the good act of one man brings everyone life,
and makes them justified.
Though we are condemned in Adam,
in Christ we are made free from condemnation.

DP:3

Again,
as by one man's disobedience many were made
    sinners,
so by one man's obedience many will be made
    righteous.
In Adam, we all have sinned;
In Christ we are made holy.

Through St Paul God is inviting us
to turn away from being like Adam,
to turn away from sin;
and instead to become more like Christ, to become
'Christ' through baptism.
Let us listen again to the words of St Paul,
without commentary this time:

Sin entered the world . . .

Key words of
contrast stressed

Repetition of key
message:
purposeful
redundancy

Dividing pause:
three seconds

Key words of
contrast stressed

Repetition of key
message
purposeful
redundancy

Repetition of
key message

Repeat text, with
only minor
modifications

APPENDIX
QUESTIONS LECTORS ASK

APPENDIX
QUESTIONS LECTORS ASK

QUESTIONS OF PRINCIPLE

Are all these techniques really necessary?
Is it not enough to read clearly and distinctly the text given, without adding anything?
If any explanation is needed, surely it ought to happen in the homily?

The commonest objections raised against the techniques that this book proposes are based on two presumptions:
—that the readings should be read word for word as they are in the Lectionary/Bible without any modifications;
—that any necessary explanation, decoding, etc., should come within the homily.

The reply is twofold:
— there is nothing sacred about the readings apart from their **meaning.** Borrowing Augustine's idea, we might describe the reading as the 'sacrament' of God's Word: the external sign of the internal message. The external words, the script itself, the sound that proclaims the words, the actual ceremonies of proclaiming the text; all these are important only in as much as they convey the meaningful message which God speaks to us through them.

We are being unfaithful to God's Word if we simply proclaim it without any regard for whether or not we are transmitting a message that can be understood: remember Charlemagne's liturgy of the Word? Our duty is to achieve maximum intelligibility of the text — to make sure that nothing comes between God speaking to his people and their receiving his message.

If the meaning of the text is the important thing, then anything which is within our power to guarantee the transmission of that meaning is justifiable.

Remember that this book is concerned with the ministry of the Word, as a whole, and not limited to strictly liturgical proclamation of the Word. If we limit ourselves to consider the Sunday celebration of the liturgy of the Word, then of the two techniques proposed to you in this book, I would expect 'simple guided reading' to be the more appropriate. However, if in certain circumstances the reading or readings will only mean something if we use the 'commentated reading' technique, then it ought to be used. This brings us to the second criticism.

— an explanation which comes after the reading will not serve the purpose. It comes too late. If the necessary decoding has not been done before, people will not understand the reading; and if they do not understand it, how are they to remember it well enough for any commentary that is to follow? It is rather like first serving your guests indigestible food, and then offering them medicine to help them digest it. The necessary explanation should be provided before the text is read or during the reading itself; only if the message has been properly grasped can it serve as a basis for the homily.

You suggest that difficult words in the text should be substituted by equivalents which are easier to understand: is this not watering down the message?

As long as the substitutions are truly 'equivalents', in other words, as long as the reader translates properly, then there is no 'watering-down'. Watering-down implies a diminution in the meaning of the original: it is exactly that original meaning that the reader seeks to express by substituting equivalents.

Is there not a danger that people will confuse the words of scripture with the words which are merely the reader's?

There might be a danger of such confusion in commentated reading, but it can be avoided with the following simple precautions:
—make it clear that you are going to read with explanations;
—include as many explicit statements to distinguish the text from your explanation 'this means . . .'

—the way you read, intonation, etc., should help distinguish text from commentary;

—when commentating, be scrupulously careful to interpret the direct meaning of the passage;

—conclude with an uncommentated reading of the passage.

QUESTIONS OF PRACTICE

Some questions are concerned not with objecting to the principles, but with how they are to be worked out in practice:

If each reading is introduced, commentated, then we have a sermon — is this not lengthening Mass unnecessarily?

This question is often asked out of sad experience, where the celebrant introduces the theme of the day with a summary of the readings; he introduces the readings, summarising them in his own words; the readings are read; the same message is repeated again in the homily.

This problem arises out of a failure to distinguish the distinct purpose of each of the times when the celebrant (or a minister) may intervene. It is important to see in what way the practical techniques proposed in this book differ from the other seemingly similar commentary opportunities in the course of a liturgical celebration:

they are distinct from opening words which may follow the greeting at the opening of the celebration. The Roman Missal advises that 'the priest or other suitable minister may very briefly introduce the Mass of the day.' *(IGMR 29).* It should be short, should flow out of the welcome of the people which precedes it, and should flow into the call to repentance which follows it;

they are distinct from the homily, which follows the readings, and so presupposes they have been understood. The homily 'should develop some point of the readings or of another text from the Ordinary or the Mass of the day. The homilist should keep in mind the mystery that is being celebrated and the needs of the particular community.' *(IGMR 41).* In other words, it should lead the people on to a deeper reflection on their own lives in the light of what they have heard in the readings. It does not repeat the message of the readings again, but presupposes the readings and draws conclusions from them. It speaks directly about how to apply them in practice to the particular community.

The introductions which 'simple guided reading' would add duplicate neither of these other liturgical functions. They are not to summarise the readings that follow, but simply and briefly to provide the information the audience needs to know to understand the scripture text.

That the functions are distinct is underlined by the fact that each may be the responsibility of a different liturgical minister: the opening words by the president or celebrant; the introduction to the scripture reading by the lector/reader; the homily by the deacon, or the celebrant. In a good liturgical celebration there will be no duplication of either ministry or function: they should complement each other in a way that helps to make the celebration a 'sacrament of unity'.

We already have a rota of readers lay readers in our parish, but very few, if any, could introduce or explain the reading in the way you describe. What should we do?

In the first place we should remember that people who cannot read properly — and normally proper reading includes explaining the text — should not be allowed to become readers at all. In their enthusiasm to involve the laity in the liturgy some parish priests have been too lenient in this regard. Certainly, the laity should be encouraged to take what is their rightful place by virtue of their baptism, which includes their right and duty to read God's Word; but they should only be allowed to do so in a public way if they are able to transmit God's Word effectively.

If people are inaudible, or unintelligible, or are known from experience not to prepare their reading, then they should not be allowed to read. No one should be allowed to read for purely diplomatic reasons, or out of etiquette or sentiment. None of us would dream of substituting beer for wine for the liturgy of the eucharist, merely because beer is easier to obtain, or to please a certain benefactor. Respect for the sacrament imposes minimum requirements on the way it is celebrated. Similarly, respect for the sacrament of God's Word imposes certain minimum requirements as regards the quality of its proclamation.

There is a danger of underestimating the capabilities of many of our lay-readers. More of them than we might at first think are well qualified to undertake the simple guided or commentated reading. Many are prepared to undergo whatever training the diocese or parish is able to provide. With proper guidance and a little insight, they will be able to prepare the readings properly. It may be that rather than readers not living up to our expectations, our expectations have been too low: experience shows that they will respond if we first show confidence in their ability.

It can happen, of course, that a reading is particularly difficult, and the reader, however competent in other ways, feels he cannot properly introduce or explain it himself. The proper thing to do is to consult the celebrant: he may be able to give enough advice or insight for the reader to work out his own explanation; alternatively, the celebrant himself may provide the explanation, which might then be read by the reader or spoken by the celebrant himself at the appropriate moment before the reading itself.

What about long and difficult readings? Sometimes the reading may be so complicated that it needs a commentary, but the commentary would make it too long — what should happen?

In such circumstances, only part of the reading should be used. This is a pastoral decision to be taken in consultation with all the liturgical ministers concerned. It is better that the people have a short reading which is properly explained and which they can understand clearly, than to have a longer text which is beyond them.

The Lectionary itself often proposes longer and shorter versions of the same reading (for example, on the 3rd, 4th and 5th Sundays of Lent, Year A, shorter forms of the gospel are given).

What about dramatised reading?

Dramatised reading can be very effective, and indeed is part of the tradition of the Church's liturgy — you will find that Passion for use on Palm Sunday (the synoptics) and Good Friday (St John) is given with the three traditional voices (the voice of narrator, of 'Christ', and of others').

Well done, it cannot but make a deep impression on the hearers. However, a multiplicity of readers will not make up for the lack of quality in the reading itself. Reading this way demands more preparation, not less; over and above the individual preparation by each of the readers involved, there has to be a full and careful rehearsal.

What about the sung proclamation of the readings, as used to happen in the pre-Vatican II sung High Mass?

The proclamation of the reading in song is one way in which the Church showed respect for the readings as the Word of God, and given certain conditions, there is no reason why this tradition should not be continued in our vernacular liturgy:

—the art of music should be entirely subject to the purpose of transmitting God's Word.

—the singing must never obscure the clarity of the message (which might happen because the singing is poorly done, or because it is so well done that it is listened to for the music and not for the message).

From a more positive point of view, if the preparatory study of a text reveals to you that the original context of the passage was to be sung, then, all other things being equal, it would be eminently appropriate to present it to the people in a sung form. For example, in his letter to the Philippians, Paul uses what is quite clearly a hymn (2:6-11).

The pastoral principles and practicalities of such singing are beyond the scope of this book — they concern the ministry of cantor rather than that of lector — other than to say that nothing can be more conducive to making God's Word speak to our minds and hearts than a competent and striking presentation of it song.

> In the presence of the men and women,
> and children old enough to understand,
> Ezra the scribe read from the book
> from early morning till noon;
> all the people listened attentively
> to the Book of the Law.
> Ezra stood on a wooden dais
> erected for the purpose.
> He read from the Law of God,
> translating and giving the sense,
> so that the people understood what was read.
>
> *(Nehemiah 8:3ff.)*